Great Americana

Eight Months in Illinois

William Oliver

those who see unavoidable difficulty approaching them, and such as have families without any adequate provision for them." But even these persons ought not think that by crossing the Atlantic they would suddenly enjoy a life of ease. "All must labour there, as well as in this country; the difference is, that, in America there is plenty of room and abundant remuneration for labour; whilst in Britain, the working population exceeds the demand, and, consequently, the price of labour is small."

Oliver had come to the Illinois country by way of New York, Philadelphia, Pittsburgh, Wheeling, Cincinnati, and Kaskaskia. He returned via St. Louis, Indianapolis, Columbus, Sandusky, and Buffalo. However he also provided his readers with other possible routes to Illinois and he gave calculations of the mileage together with the probable expense of each. In concentrating his attention on the state of Illinois, Oliver explained that he did so not because he necessarily recommended it over the other states but simply because it was the region he knew best in the United States.

Among the topics which he discussed at some length were: the purchase of lands in

Eight Months in Illinois

by William Oliver

READEX MICROPRINT

Fo

In December of 1841, William
Englishman, set out from New Yor
trip to the Midwest which allov
spend several months in the state
Upon his return to England so ma
interested in emigrating to America
him about conditions there that h
publish an account of what he ha
"poorer classes" in England wei
whom he wrote primarily. Althou
Months In Illinois; With Informa
grants (published in 1843) cont
variety of information about life i
is especially valuable for its pic
nomic conditions in the state of

Oliver warned his fellow co
weigh any decision to emigrate
man whose prospects at home w
better stay there. Emigration was

31

Illinois, the agricultural possibilities of the region, and the general economic outlook. Yet he also analyzed the kind of society an emigrant would find in Illinois, the character of the people, their religion, and the educational and cultural opportunities open to them.

Oliver conscientiously pointed out both the good and the bad features of life in Illinois. Although he pronounced the western prairies as "beyond doubt the most healthy" for settlers, he admitted, for example, that the discomfort caused by insects was no trifling matter. "The whole earth and air seems teeming with them, and mosquitos, gallinippers, bugs, ticks, sand-flies, sweat-flies, house-flies, ants, cockroaches, &c., join in one continued attack against one's ease."

More background about the author is included in an editor's note to William Oliver, *Eight Months in Illinois* (Chicago, 1924), pp. 5-6. To compare Oliver's description with those provided in other books written for emigrants see Ralph Leslie Rusk, *The Literature of the Middle Western Frontier* (New York, 1962), I, 79-130.

EIGHT MONTHS

IN

ILLINOIS;

WITH

INFORMATION TO EMIGRANTS.

BY WILLIAM OLIVER.

The pride to rear an independent shed,
And give the lips we love unborrow'd bread ;
To see a world from shadowy forests won,
In youthful beauty wedded to the sun ;
To skirt our home with harvests widely sown,
And call the blooming landscape all our own,
Our children's heritage in prospect long.
These are the hopes, high-minded hopes, and strong,
That beckon England's wanderers o'er the brine,——

THOMAS CAMPBELL.

NEWCASTLE UPON TYNE:

PRINTED BY WILLIAM ANDREW MITCHELL,

AND SOLD BY

E. & T. BRUCE, GREY STREET; W. EASTON, JEDBURGH;

AND J. D. KENNEDY, HAWICK.

———

MDCCCXLIII.

INSCRIBED

TO

THE LABOURING MEN OF ROXBURGHSHIRE,

WITH SINCERE WISHES

FOR

THEIR WELFARE.

PREFACE.

In commencing the arrangement of the following notes, the principal object the author had in view was to afford as much information as possible, in a shape that might be available to the poorer classes. The volume, however, though small, and published in a cheap form, has attained to a size which he did not anticipate,—a circumstance which may in some measure defeat his object; still he is inclined to think that there is very little contained in it which does not, more or less, tend to throw some light either on the people or on the country of which it treats.

It may be said that there is no need of books on America— an assertion which, as regards certain classes, may be true; but many of the books on that country are expensive, and no single work on Illinois, with which the author is acquainted, enters sufficiently into details for the poor emigrant.

The information given has, to a considerable extent, been determined by enquiries made of the author by intending emigrants, and whilst he thinks there may be found information useful to such, he at the same time hopes that the work may not be entirely destitute of the means of affording amusement to the general reader.

LANGRAW, 12th August, 1843.

CONTENTS.

CHAPTER I.

CHAPTER II.

CHAPTER III.

CHAPTER IV.

CHAPTER V.

CHAPTER VI.

CHAPTER VII.

CHAPTER VIII.

EIGHT MONTHS IN ILLINOIS,

&c.

CHAPTER I.

AFTER remaining a week in New York, a friend and I started for *the West* before daylight, on a morning of the first week of December. A brisk wind swept along the deserted streets, and the cold was so intense, we had to move along with all the speed we could exert, to prevent ourselves from being frozen. On arriving at the station from which the steamboat started, we were introduced into a crowded room, whose atmosphere was at a temperature so different from that without, as to cause a feeling almost of suffocation. After a short time all were on board, and the boat started.

On the approach of daylight, I became aware that the boat was crowded with passengers, who, so long as it was dark, had kept themselves quiet on benches, chairs, and tables, or ensconced in any quiet nook, clear of the disturbance of passing feet. No sooner, however, were there signs of preparation for breakfast, than all were on the alert, taking up their ground most systematically for the onslaught. I had already seen some rushing and scrambling at meals, in hotels and boarding-houses, but the affair was somewhat differently managed in the boat; the seats, ranged along each side of the cabin, were gradually occupied, till the two expectant rows were sitting at open order, so that the servants could, without much interruption, bring forward the materials of attack. No sooner did the first chime of the warning bell sound through the boat, than the ranks simultaneously closed in upon the table, and the attack commenced, and proceeded with a vigour known only in this country. Some trifling impediments there were at the commencement from a lack of plates, when two hands might be seen attempting to urge one of these articles in contrary directions; but all and each minded the main chance with such a will, that there were no hindrances of any moment. My friend had secured his plate, but imprudently quitted hold of it, in order to attack a fowl at no great distance; which fowl, however, just as he was about to secure it, eluded his grasp. Thinking the gentleman who had taken it would be content with cutting off a portion, and handing back the rest, he patiently waited, and received the bones, after they had undergone the inspection of another person, who apparently thought them not worth having; when, lo, he found he had nothing to receive them upon: his right hand neighbour having been in want of a plate, had, without saying by your leave, taken his. The look of mixed surprise and chagrin which he cast me, on sustaining this double misfortune, gave rise to an emotion of the ludicrous, which, however, was instantly chilled down by the state of the social atmosphere by which we were surrounded. There was no talking: everything was done with the most imperturbable gravity. Space had been left at the head of the table for the ladies, who, on rising, retired to their cabin from which they had issued at the commencement of the meal.

At Amboy, about 25 miles from New York, we were transferred to the Camden and Amboy Railroad, by which we were conveyed a distance of 33½ miles, through a somewhat poorlooking country, to Bordentown, on the Delaware river, and from thence by steamboat, 29 miles down the river to Philadelphia.

The Delaware is here a broad placid river, and must look beautiful in summer. Its banks are enlivened by many picturesque buildings and some nice villages. But there was small opportunity of marking the beauties of the scenery on a boat rushing at a speed of 15 miles an hour, through an atmosphere nearly at zero.

Philadelphia is a fine city, regularly built, with wide streets, embellished in many places with beautiful shade trees, planted at intervals along the outer edge of the footway. It is situated at the south-east point of Pensylvania, on a neck of land between the Schuylkill and Delaware rivers. The population in 1830 was 167,811, and in 1840, 258,832, shewing an increase during the last ten years of 91,021.

There are very extensive beds and veins of anthracite coal in the neighbouring districts, particularly at Pottsville, at the head of the Schuylkill canal, a distance of 106 miles, and at Mauch Chunk, on the Lehigh, a distance of 108 miles by water from Philadelphia.

Left Philadelphia for Pittsburg by railway, (the only route at this season, when the canal boats have been laid up for winter,) and passed through a well-inhabited country, with good houses, barns, &c., and in general, with an appearance of comfort and stability not surpassed, I am inclined to think, in many sections of the union. Among the inhabitants are many Dutch, or of Dutch extraction, a people the least given to change, perhaps, of any in the world. They have brought with them, from their father-land, their habits of economy and industry, and amongst other things, the pointed gables and weathercocks.

On arriving at Harrisburg, the capital of the state, our railway travelling was at an end, as that means of conveyance was not completed any farther, so that we had to adopt the only remaining one at this season, to wit, *the stage.* Conceive a huge clumsy article, somewhat like a boat, slung on leather straps, and surrounded between the roof and what may be termed the gunwale with oilcloth hangings, instead of panels. There is a seat at each end, and one in the middle, opposite the doors, with a leather strap stretched across as a support for such passengers as are so unlucky as to be doomed to this seat. Seats are not, as with us, retained by the first occupant; of course, there is a good deal of manœuvreing to obtain such as are considered most comfortable. The ladies, however, are always allowed to choose. The number of human beings engulphed in this, the first of these vehicles I set my foot in, was twelve.

I shall not attempt to describe the vicissitudes of travel, unintermitted, except at meals and change of horses, during nearly three days and three nights; suffice it to say, that, after performing a number of marvellous flying leaps, plunging through slashes, where our vehicle floundered about like some unwieldy monster of the deep in shoal water; going at one time at a hand gallop to acquire the impetus necessary for clearing some difficulty, at another, proceeding with the utmost caution for fear of being precipitated from the ice-covered track into some ravine, we at length arrived at Pittsburg, completely tired, and glad to have escaped from the stage, and from the snow and intense frost of the Alleghanies. Of the scenery on our route, I can say very little, as most of what is considered the finest was passed in the night; and during the day the curtains were kept closed, on account of the cold.

The Susquehanna, about Harrisburg, is a magnificent, clear river; its broad reaches, where exposed to the eye, looking beautiful in the dark setting of the forest. Unlike the western rivers, it is varied by pool and stream rolling over a gravelly bottom; and for some time before arriving at, and after leaving Harrisburg, we heard the sound of its waters, caused, I believe, by some rocky rapids in the neighbourhood.

About eight miles above Harrisburg, we crossed the Susquehanna in a ferry-boat, and could see, between us and the sky, some portions of a viaduct in the course of being erected for the railway. Our course now lay up the Juniatta river, until we reached the mountains, which, in this part of the range, are not very grand, on account of the gradual ascent from the sea;—indeed, in many places, they appear more like the effects of the watercourses in a high range of country, than mountains according to the European acceptation of the word. We had, however, some glimpses of very imposing scenery, though very seldom a view of any great extent. We sometimes came upon the canal, as it wound its way along the watercourses and ravines. Some snow fell, and there was reason to fear that our progress would be impeded; but the weather became calm, with hard frost. Before reaching Pittsburg, the country became animated by numbers of comfortable-looking farm-houses, and well-cleared fields.

Pittsburg is situated at the point of land at the junction of the Monongahela and Alleghany rivers, and is distant by water 965 miles from the Mississippi, and 2003 miles from New Orleans. It is a place of importance, and one of the grand keys between the eastern and western states, being at the head of the steamboat navigation from the west. Another cause of prosperity exists in a plentiful supply of coal, by which it has become a place of considerable importance in the manufacture of iron-ware, &c. The seams of coal are in the bluffs of the Monongahela, and on the opposite side from Pittsburg, at an elevation of about 320 feet from the water. Drifts are made directly into the face of the bluff, and the coals are lowered down the almost perpendicular descent to the river, by means of reciprocating cars running on a railway. There is an excellent wooden bridge over each river. Although the boating season was nearly over, I counted 30 steamers at the lèvee. There were lately between 80 and 90 steam-engines at work in the city and its neighbourhood. The population, in 1830, was 12,542, and in 1840, was 21,296; the latter number referring only to Pittsburg proper. The suburbs and villages connected with the city are very populous.

Few things are more surprising, to a native of the old country, on examining some of the western towns, even of recent date, than the multitude of articles of luxury, which he meets with in the stores and warerooms. He may have toiled all day, through the tracts in the primeval forest, without seeing a live thing, except, perhaps, a deer or a squirrel, and come upon a town, stuck down among the woods, with the undecayed stumps in its streets, and there, where he might suppose it hopeless to expect anything beyond the bare necessaries of life, he will find stores containing many of the luxuries of cities long settled in civilization. I saw at Pittsburg a large wareroom full of upholstery and cabinet work, consisting of elegant mahogany tables and chairs, sofas, chests of drawers, bureaus, work-tables, pianofortes, &c. At every step one encounters the anomaly of semi-barbarism joined with civilized existence.

Having stayed two days at Pittsburg, I went to the levee, and found two boats about to start down the river. These were likely to be the last boats for the season, and there evidently being an understanding between the captains, I had to submit to an overcharge. The cabin fare charged to Cincinnati, 460 miles, was 15 dollars ; about one-third more than the ordinary charge.

The frost had been intense for some days, and there was a good deal of floating ice on the Alleghany. A few days more, it was asserted, would bind up the Ohio firm and fast. The rivers were low too, so low that none, except the smallest craft, could pass the bars and sand banks in the Ohio. Luckily, ours was a small boat. Under these somewhat discouraging circumstances, we swung round from the levee, and commenced our run down "La belle riviere," skirting an immense circular field of floating ice, revolving with the water, at the junction of the rivers. The Ohio is here 600 yards wide. We were soon satisfied that the fears entertained of the lowness of the river were not without reason, as the boat several times rasped against the bottom.

Everything about a western steamer, from the boat to the passengers inclusive, appears novel to an old country man. The boat is a slight thing, fitted only for inland navigation, and whose hull forms a comparatively small portion of the fabric. Immediately above the water line, or what would constitute the gunwale of the hull itself, spars about four feet long are laid horizontally ; thus increasing the width by eight feet. On this deck are situated the furnaces, boilers, and engine. The boilers are cylinders, proportioned in size to the power wanted, and five or

six in number, are ranged across the beam, the furnaces opening on the forecastle. The engine is placed immediately behind
the boilers, the piston working horizontally, and, with the inter-
vention of a joint, directly on the crank of the paddle shaft. I
never noticed a boat with more than one engine, and that invariably high pressure. This deck is partially shut in by places
for cooking, larders, storerooms, &c., and to it the steerage passengers are restricted, their locale being abaft the engine; and a
higgledy piggledy place it is when full of passengers.

Immediately above this is the cabin deck, which is divided into
three apartments, the ladies' cabin farthest aft, the gentlemen's
cabin, which is also the dining-room, and the bar, which very
appropriately is over the boilers. The staterooms, which contain two berths each, are ranged along the sides of the cabin,
and, in many boats, have doors which open to a sort of gangway, on which a fellow in hot nights may take a promenade *in
puris;* no small luxury when mosquitos are not troublesome.

The cabin is covered in by what is termed the hurricane deck,
which is resorted to as a promenade, and on which, overlooking
the forcastle, is situated the pilot's house, a small square apart-
ment, roofed in, and glazed all round to within about four feet
of the deck. In this is the wheel, which acts on the rudder by
means of ropes or chains led aft. In this position, the steersman
can readily see and avoid many obstructions, such as floating
trees, &c., which it would be impossible for him to do in the
ordinary position. Indeed the improvement is so obvious, at least
to my uunautical experience, that I am surprised it is not adopted
in some shape among our own river craft.

There are placards hanging in every boat, with a list of regulations, some of which appear rather odd to a stranger. Among
the regulations on one of the boats, I saw two which I thought
worthy of notice, the one intimating that if "any of the boats'
servants committed a fault, gentlemen would be kind enough not
to chastise them with their own hand, but would complain of
them to the officers of the boat;" the other, that "gentlemen
would be kind enough not to turn into the beds with their boots
on." The gentlemen evaded the enactment against the boots by
turning in their bodies, and leaving their legs and boots sticking
out.

The gambling on some of these boats is frightful; indeed, it is
said that many individuals make a profession of it, and are constantly travelling on the rivers. It is whispered, too, that some
of these take still more unwarrantable means than gambling to
possess themselves of their neighbour's property, and that some-

times a passenger goes on board a boat who is never seen nor heard of again. "Every one," to quote what I heard remarked, "every one is armed with a bowie knife or some weapon—when there is no moon, the summer nights are very dark in these latitudes, and the sound of the paddle wheels would prevent a plunge in the river from being heard."

As the ice still continued to increase, we were apprehensive that the boat would be unable to proceed. The speed was much slackened, and one morning the boat had to make way through a continued sheet of ice, which, it was asserted, another night's frost would render impregnable ; luckily, however, a thaw commenced, and we saw no more ice on the Ohio.

At Wheeling, we were detained an entire day, waiting for the chance of passengers expected by a stage from Baltimore ; the great national road from that city striking the river here.— Great discontent prevailed amongst the passengers, but they evidently never dreamed of making any remonstrance.

Wheeling, in Virginia, is a thriving place, with a population of between five and six thousand. The bluffs in the neighbourhood are bold and abounding in coal.

The expected stage arrived, and we got some additional passengers, among the rest a southern planter, a man of very gentlemanly address and pleasing manners. I mention this, because I was struck with it at the time. I had not anticipated such a marked difference between the people of the eastern and southern states. This, of course, was only one example, but future experience confirmed the opinion I then imbibed. The southern man seems to have applied to his head some of the time which he of the east applies almost exclusively to his purse. Whilst the down-easter takes for his motto "go ahead," and acts accordingly, he of the south appears meditative, and inclined to enjoy the *otium cum dignitate*. They are both thinking men ; but the one is a clever, shrewd man of the world, whilst the other has a much more circumscribed intercourse with his fellows, and is in some degree a man of retirement. The one will ask the price of produce down east, and will exhibit amongst strangers a cold and forbidding exterior ; the other will talk to you of his conservatory and of his flowers, and will carry along with him some of the feelings and amenities of home. Both are kind and hospitable at their own hearths. There is, perhaps, more classification of society in the south than in the east, and I here allude to a portion of the higher class, if such distinction may be allowed in America. What may be termed the lower class, in the slave states, seems tinctured with a rudeness, in some instances amounting to ferocity, which is very repulsive.

Let no foreigner, when travelling on the western waters, or, indeed, in any part of the U. S., enter into discussions on the slave question, unless he is sure that he is amongst friends, as the state of excitement, particularly in the slave states, is such, that it would often be dangerous to support either the abolitionists or their opponents. I have seen half the passengers in a boat very much excited, some of them perfectly infuriated, on the subject of slavery; but then, it very conveniently happened, that they were all on one side. One man rose from his seat, stamping on the floor, and throwing his arms about, in a paroxysm of fury against the abolitionists. "Who can endure it?" he cried: "Were they not bought by our money, or inherited from our fathers? Are they not, therefore, as much our property as anything else in our possession? They are not equal to the white man, but are intermediate between him and the brute creation, and were made for the express purpose of being slaves. I speak feelingly, for I have suffered. I was a post-master in Alabama. Some of the gentlemen in my district suspected that intercourse by letter was carried on between that and some other part of the country on the subject of slavery, and they requested me to open suspicious letters, which I did, and I still think I did right, although it cost me my situation. Disgusted at such injustice, I determined on leaving the state, and on going to one where there were no slaves. I went to Indiana; but it will not do, there is no getting any one to work, no getting along. I have sold all off, and am now on my way back to Alabama."

Whilst on the subject of slavery, I here subjoin an extract from an American work, purporting to be impartial in its information on that question. "As it regards the condition of slaves in the United States, it will be safe to say that they are generally well fed, comfortably clad, and not overwrought or unmercifully chastised. It is the interest of all masters, and the inclination of most, to see that their bondmen do not suffer. They have cabins of their own, and are usually allowed a day, or part of a day, per week, to work for themselves. In sickness they are cared for, and in their old age they are not thrust forth to perish. Many of them are employed as house servants, the rest labour in the field under overseers, who see that they attend to their business, and chastise the idle and refractory. It is believed that very many of the slaves, perhaps one half, knowing no other condition, are contented and happy. Many are ardently attached to their masters. Still, disguise it as we will, slavery is 'a bitter draught.' Wherever one man has unlimited power over another, there is at least a liability to abuse it, and hence the insurrections which have disturbed the tranquillity of the south so often. Hence the murders committed by masters upon slaves, and by slaves upon masters. Hence the enormities recorded in every newspaper. Hence the advertisements for runaways; and hence it is that the people of South Carolina have built a citadel in their capital to which they may fly for refuge in case of insurrection.

" The evils to which the whites are liable in consequence of holding slaves are mainly these—insecurity of life and property, the bad habits attendant on idleness, ruin of their lands, great expense with little proportionate return, strife with their neighbours, depravation of their own and their children's morals.

" The evils to which the slave is but too subject, are as follows : With the feelings, passions, and intellect of a man, he is, in the social system, a mere chattle, or at best, a brute. He is without the protection of law, without having committed any crime. He may be bought and sold, or given away, or lost at a horse race or gambling table. He may he scourged or tortured, as the caprice of any white man may dictate, without the possibility of redress. Husbands and wives, parents and children may be torn asunder, and driven into separate bondage, whenever it so pleases their owner. There is no protection for the chastity of woman. The slave can hold no property, however industrious. He can make no contracts. He cannot be a party or witness in any suit in which a white man is concerned, however much he may have been injured. He cannot purchase his freedom. In some states, his owner is not permitted, by law, to emancipate him without the consent of his creditors, or on condition of sending him out of the land. In Georgia, the master is punished for emancipating. In Virginia, if a slave make a bargain, he is publicly whipped for it : at least such is the law. The law sets no limit to the chastisement the slave may receive from his master. In Georgia and North Carolina, if a negro ' die of moderate correction,' the law bears the master harmless. In South Carolina, a white who kills a slave may purge himself by his own oath. Slaves are forbidden to learn to read and write, and punished for disobedience by patrols, or officers appointed for the purpose. They may not meet for religious worship, on pain of being dispersed and whipped. Whites are fined and whipped for teaching them, and in Louisiana may in some cases be imprisoned for life, or put to death. There are few legal marriages of slaves, because the tie is not respected. A slave is punished with whipping for teaching the gospel, and, in Virginia, he may be put to death for practising medicine. Such are a portion of the ills to which the slave is heir. Perhaps all these severe liabilities may be justified by necessity or expediency; but that they exist, is proved by the statutes of all the slave-holding states, and cases under each of the above general heads are of frequent occurrence. Slave-holders and abolitionists are at issue on each and every one of them, and these are a few of the arguments adduced on both sides.

"'We acknowledge,' say the former, 'that slavery is a foul blot on our country's fame, and that it is contrary to justice and the law of God. We deplore it deeply, but what can we do? The system was entailed on us by Great Britain, and we cannot get rid of it. If we set our bondmen free, they will plunder and murder us. Religion and education make them discontented with their condition, and therefore it is unsafe to let them have either. Besides, were they free, they are so ignorant and lazy, that they neither could nor would maintain themselves; they would rather starve than work. We could not do without them, for white men cannot sustain the heat of our climate. If we allow them to possess property, they will soon be our equals, and sharers in our property and soil. They are destitute of intelligence, and appear to have been formed by nature for servitude. We treat them well, and they are contented. They would not accept freedom, were it offered, and they are infinitely better off than the free labourers in the northern states. If free, they would amalgamate with us. Above all, they are our property, guaranteed to us by the constitution, and if you take them from us, you wrong us. You have no right to meddle with the matter, and if you do, we will secede from the union.'

"The abolitionists answer, 'If you acknowledge that your conduct is unjust and disgraceful, and displeasing to God, cease from it. You ought to scorn to hold an inheritance of sin and disgrace from Great Britain. If you deplore the evil, show your sorrow by action. You can get rid of it if you choose. Your slaves will not murder you for doing them justice; but they will if you withhold it. If their ignorance makes them dangerous, how can religion and education have the same effect? The experience of other countries does not justify you in apprehending any danger from emancipation. They now maintain themselves and you too; surely they can maintain themselves alone. In other countries where negroes have been emancipated, they have not starved. You say you cannot work in your country. Have you tried? If you cannot, you have no business there. If they acquire property by their industry, why should they not have it? They do so in the north, and no one complains. If they are inferior to yourselves in intellect, it is no reason that you should oppress them, but rather the contrary, and the fact itself is not proved. If you treat them well, and they love you, why do you fear them? and why do so many run away? Offer them freedom, and see if they will not accept it. It is not true that their condition is preferable, or by any means equal, to the free labourers in the north. It is true that if you give them freedom, they will amalgamate with you, and so they will if they remain in bondage. Half the people in the United States are mulattoes already. No constitution, no human law can authorise manifest wrong. We have a right to advise you, and you know better than to secede from the union.'

"These arguments have been extracted almost indiscriminately from the printed papers of both parties. It is hard to tell what judgment to form on the matter; but if a little more forbearance were shown on both sides, it would do no harm. The question involves so many interests, that all the combined wisdom of the nation might be at a loss to reconcile them. May Divine Providence remove the evil from our land without injustice to any one."

We left Wheeling, and were once more on our way down the river, calling at almost every town on the route, receiving or landing passengers and freight. Some of the towns are finely situated, though many of them may be called towns in embryo, and all must yield precedence to Cincinnati, " the Queen of the West," where we arrived without meeting with anything worthy of notice.

About half a century ago, the place on which the city now stands was a wilderness, without a white inhabitant. In 1813, it contained about 4,000 inhabitants; in 1820, 10,000; in 1830, 24,831; and in 1840, 46,382.

There is a good deal of manufacture of various kinds in Cincinnati, and many extensive grist and saw mills, worked by steam power. The American work formerly referred to, gives a list, amongst other things, of " 24 Churches, the College, Athenæum, Medical College, Mechanic's Institute, four Market Houses, a Theatre, two Museums, *a famous and casteless Bazaar*, Banks, Court House, &c." There are between 15 and 20 periodical publications.

The lèvee is high and steep, and is one of the best on the river; it is, however, exposed to the current, which causes boats arriving and leaving frequently to run foul of those lying there. The river is about half a mile wide.

The country in the neighbourhood of Cincinnati is populous,

and there are many fine farms. Land in the immediate neighbourhood is very dear, and at a distance of five or six miles,
sells for 40 or 50 dollars an acre. An immense number of
hogs are annually slaughtered in the city, and shipped down the
river for the southern states and the West Indies.

Louisville, in Kentucky, 131 miles below Cincinnati, is a place
of considerable commercial importance, perhaps most so of any
place on the Ohio, with a population of about 15,000. It is
situated at the falls or rapids, which, when the river is low,
obstruct the navigation. To obviate this, a canal two miles in
length has been cut, which ensures a passage to the largest class
of steamers. The river had here risen about fifteen feet perpendicular, owing to the freshet which had taken place after our
leaving Pittsburg.

There are few places of much consequence between this and
the mouth of the river, which now begins to lose its bluffs, perhaps from their receding to such a distance as to be no longer
discernible; the view, of consequence, becomes less picturesque,
being bounded on either hand by a dark forest of lofty timber,
and the solitude is complete, nothing being heard save the hoarse
intermittent roar of the steam from the escape-funnel reverbe-
rating through the lifeless woods with a wearisome monotony.

Farther up the country, and whilst the river is passing the
states of Virginia and Kentucky on the one side, and those of
Ohio and Indiana on the other, the scenery is often very beautiful, and the boat glides through the clear and placid waters,
passing many fair islands and romantic bluffs. The large alluvial bottoms, teeming with fertility, are full of thriving, well-
cleared farms, and comfortable-looking brick houses, with the
never-failing accompaniment of a well-stored orchard. Flocks
of sheep, particularly in Ohio, are seen grazing in the fields and
on the sloping bluffs, and the tinkling of the cow-bell everywhere
meets the ear. When it can be accomplished, the houses are
often built on the top of the bluff, the situation being considered
healthier than in the bottom, and many so placed have fine meadows in front, sweeping down to the margin of the broad river.
Plenty seems here to have scattered the choicest treasures of
her horn.

Many of the trees are very tall, and of great size; but the
sycamore, the button wood of the eastern states, is most conspi-
cuous. It thrives on the banks of rivers, and is frequently seen
on the margin, stretching its giant arms over the water. The
bark of the smaller limbs is a chalky white, mottled with pale
green. I was told that one of those trees, on an island in the
Ohio, measured upwards of 13 feet in diameter.

Many of the towns on the banks of the Ohio are little more than a name, for which the country is indebted to the speculators in town lots, who, of course, would advertise and trumpet forth the qualifications of a town in the moon, if there was a chance of selling any of the lots. Let not the traveller, when he looks at his map, and sees the name of some city hallowed by antiquity, be confident that he will find a place realizing his ideas of the original. Most likely there will be a store and spirit shop, with a bit of board stuck up, on which some one has scrawled the word HOTEL, apparently with his finger dipt in ink; with one or two log houses scattered along the river's bank.— Such were some that I saw, and among them one bearing the honoured name of Caledonia, consisting of three, or at most of four, wretched log huts, squeezed into a small clearing in the forest-wilderness. No doubt, every earthly thing must have a beginning, but some of these towns are evidently "the beginning of the end."

Before arriving at the mouth, we looked out anxiously for the Father of Waters; but could not, even after we were told he was in sight, distinguish him, until we came very near, and then it was more from the quantity of ice floating on his surface than from any local feature, that we became aware of his presence.— This results from the Ohio gradually bending, particularly on the left shore, in the direction of the course of the Mississippi.— One might readily suppose it only a bend in the river. The place of junction has the appearance of a large lake; and from the landing-place, at Bird's Point, there is a view of seven or eight miles down the Mississippi, and of nearly as much up the Ohio. The Mississippi is here one mile, and the Ohio one mile and three quarters, wide.

As the boat was bound for New Orleans, and I intended to ascend the Mississippi, I was set ashore to wait for some boat which should pass for St. Louis. The appearance of the rivers was grand, but the adjuncts were anything but agreeable. The place had a bad name, and certainly did not seem very captivating or safe, from the number of idle, vagabond-looking boatmen who were strolling about its desolate shores. These were some of the crews of a great number of flat boats or scows, which lined the shores of the Ohio, and who durst not, with such unwieldy things, venture into the ice on the Mississippi. Fortunately, there were five of us travelling the same route, and as we had become in some measure acquainted during our voyage down the Ohio, we felt the more confident. Whilst one watched the luggage, the rest went about to see if they could procure

D

accommodation at any place besides the inn, as it had anything
but a good character. We might have saved ourselves the trouble, however, as there was no other dwelling, except a log hut,
full of the choppers of wood for the steamers. We walked about
the bank till near dark, in the expectation of a boat for St. Louis,
or some other town up the Mississippi; but night approached
without any boat appearing, and we reluctantly had our things
carried to the house, which aspired to the distinction of hotel.
Two of our party, however, found one of the owners of a flat boat
whom they knew, and got themselves huddled into his boat,
amongst a cargo of horses, fowls, yankee bedposts, &c. I looked
down into their den, and how they contrived to stow themselves
away at night, along with four or five people belonging to the
boat, I do not pretend to guess. On going into the bar-room
of the inn, I was somewhat surprised to find it very much like
the bars of other inns; there were, to be sure, two or three
strange outlandish-looking gentry sitting around the stove; but
such visions are very frequently met with in all the taverns and
boats on these rivers,

CHAPTER II.

The prospect had now become rather dreary. The ice on the Mississippi was so dense, that it was very doubtful if any boat would venture into it; it was certain that no boat, except one of the strongest and most powerful, would make the attempt, and equally certain that there would be some danger and risk of losing the boat. There was no road from the point in any direction; no such thing dreamed of as a stage, nor so much as a waggon for love or money. Taking it on foot, with the chance of bivouacing in the woods for two or three nights, was the only chance of getting away. To be sure, the landlord had a horse, which he very politely offered us for three times its value, but when he "obnoxiously made his approaches," we declined the proffered favour.

All went on very well till a short time after supper, when, as we were sitting in the bar-room, two men, Kentucks, came in; one of them desiring to write a letter, the other, as ugly a looking fellow as I ever saw, standing by. The scribe had scarcely commenced, when the landlord went up to him, and enquired if he was not the person who had lately insulted him at the wood-yard. The Kentuck denied that he had done anything to insult him. "Do you not reckon it an insult, sir, said the landlord, a tall, thin fellow, with an agueish look, and a dreadful cough, to moor your flat boat at my wood-yard, where you have no right to bring it, and when I merely mentioned it to you, and cautioned you that you might get your boat staved by some of the steamers which came to the yard for firewood, do you call it no insult to threaten to put a bullet through me? If it had not been that I was alone, sir, I would have pitched you into the river." "Well, sir—now, sir," edged in the little Kentuck, "hear me, sir, will you, sir, give us the usage of a gentleman, sir—speak to us as one gentleman ought to speak to another, sir." "Yes, sir, treat us like gentlemen, sir—treat us genteelly, &c.,

&c.," said the tall, ugly Kentuck. After an immense deal of
palaver, and the most horrible swearing on both sides, for about
a quarter of an hour, the writer tore his letter to pieces, saying,
he found this was no place for gentlemen, that he would disdain
to stay in it any longer, and that he would report the landlord's
behaviour, and do all in his power to injure his custom. The
brawl had now come to such a height, and there was so much
gesticulation, that I looked every moment for the long knives,
which are very generally carried, and had serious apprehen-
sions that the fray would end in bloodshed. The Kentucks had
been gradually retreating towards the door, on attaining which,
they said somewhat I did not hear, but which so enraged our
landlord, that he rushed after them in the dark, and such a
shrieking and shouting arose, that I thought some of them had
got stabbed, particularly when one cried murder. There had
been no harm done, however, but the affair did not look much
better when the landlord came into the bar-room, took up his
rifle and carefully examined the priming, and the bar-keeper and
he began hastily to load two or three other guns and some pis-
tols. The Kentucks, having been joined by their companions at
the boat, now commenced shouting and firing guns in bravado,
to see, as I understood, if they could induce their opponents to
come out and have a regular battle; our landlord, however,
merely went to the door and fired off a pistol, to let them know
that he was prepared for them. Nothing more took place, and
in a short time all was quiet.

Next morning (it was Sunday) when I awoke, the sun was
just rising over the forest of Kentucky, and through two windows
on opposite sides of the room, I could lie in my bed and look
out on the two mighty rivers, the Ohio glittering in the rays of
the sun, and studded with immense quantities of driftwood, and
the Father of Waters covered with an almost entire mass of ice,
moving steadily along with a sort of mysterious hurtling noise,
the dense, dark forest lining the distant shore of each. There
was the stillness of death, save that sound proceeding from the
ice-clad river, and now and then the report of a gun, rolling on
till lost in the woods.

The boatmen of the numerous flat boats were mostly provided
with guns, and shot ducks on the river, or went to the woods to
shoot deer, which were in great abundance, particularly on the
Kentucky side of the Ohio. After breakfast, the whole forest
far and near seemed to be alive with men, cracking and shooting in all directions; its being Sunday, not seeming to influence
in the slightest degree these almost lawless denizens of the
western wilderness.

There was, on this day, an occurrence at Bird's Point, which I was inclined to suspect would not be frequent. A priest, of what persuasion I know not, happened to be amongst us, who, having intimated a desire to preach, was permitted by the landlord to occupy a room in the hotel. A considerable number, I think about thirty, attended, and it was strange to look round on the rough, weather-beaten, and, in some instances, savage-looking faces of the hearers. The preacher delivered a very appropriate and sensible discourse.

Another day passed in tedious expectation. The frost having become less intense, and the influence of the sun being very considerable, so much so, indeed, that some of the people walked about through the day with their coats off, the ice had grown somewhat thinner. It takes a severe frost to preserve the ice from being thawed before it reaches this latitude, 37° north.— This day two boats came down the Mississippi from St. Louis, and their report of the difficulty and danger of coming down made our case almost hopeless. The boats had come in company all the way, the one in the wake of the other, and that which had sailed foremost had not a board left on her paddle wheels. When there was such difficulty in getting down, it may easily be conceived that there would be still greater difficulty in ascending against a current of five or six miles an hour.

A boat came up the river from New Orleans, for Cincinnati, whose report rather revived us again, as she had been able, though with considerable difficulty, to make way against the ice, which, however, was thinner below than above the junction of the rivers. There was no ice on the Ohio. This boat told us of one which we might expect in a few hours, on her way to St. Louis; but night came, and no boat.

This must be a very unhealthy place, as it lies so low, that when the Mississippi rises in June, from the melting of the snow on the Rocky Mountains, it overflows almost every foot of land, all around far into the forest, and on the Mississippi, at frequent intervals, for about 30 miles up the river. The inn is set upon posts of seven or eight feet high, and is placed on the highest spot of ground in the neighbourhood, and a sort of gangway, also raised on posts, and cross logs, connects the house and store, at which is the landing place for passengers and goods, when the water is high. The landing is on the Ohio, the Mississippi being nearly a quarter of a mile from the inn.

To those who do not know the locality, it may appear singular that there is no town on this point—a fact, however, of itself sufficient to indicate the impracticability of such an undertaking,

E

No doubt a town might be built, but the whole point is composed of an alluvion so very friable, that if the Mississippi, in one of his ordinary freaks, were to change his course, the whole affair might be swept away in a few days.   Some may think of embankments, but that is a dream—the baseless fabric of a vision.   For a long way up the river there is no shore, but a perpendicular mud bank, which is constantly being undermined and tumbled into the river; besides, the whole point is liable to periodical inundation.

On the afternoon of next day (Christmas) the long-looked-for boat arrived, and we were gratified to hear her captain say he was determined to proceed.   So much time, however, was put off in fixing some trees to the bows of the boat, to ward off the ice, that night approached, and the captain thought proper not to venture into the ice till next morning.

Early next morning we started.   A considerable number of people had collected on the extreme point to witness the attempt. It certainly was with some anxiety that we saw the bows of the boat enter the ice, and the shaking and agitation caused by the striking of the paddles on the large pieces, were very considerable; we found, however, that the boat could make way, though slowly, and in a short time nobody seemed to care much about it.

The Mississippi very much differs from the Ohio in its natural features.   There is a solitary desolation that strikes one with a sense of melancholy.   Its turbid and heavily boiling appearance—the ruinous banks, constantly tumbling in along with quantities of trees—the low, swampy character of much of the country on each side—the enormous quantities of driftwood, jammed and piled high on the upper points of the numerous islands—the uninteresting sameness and apparent instability of these islands—the total want of everything like the marks of civilization, except at wide intervals, and then a poor log hut, looking insignificant amid the mightiness of the silent forest, with a few individuals crawling about with listless sickly countenances, apparently uninterested by anything under the sun, and the idea that they may be the very refuse of humanity, driven from the bosom of society on account of their crimes, originate anything but pleasant sensations.   There is a grandeur, but it is the grandeur of desolation.

In trying to avoid the ice, the pilot ran the boat aground; she was got off, however, after a short time.   Not long after we ran bump against a snag, which made the boat reel again, and as a climax, before many hours we were aground again, firm and fast, and lay a long time, in spite of all exertions to get off. The wheels were backed with all the power of the engine, some combustible matter being thrown into the furnaces, and all the passengers were mustered on the storm deck, and marched from one side to the other, in order to loosen her hold on the mud.—After puffing and blowing till I thought they would blow her up, the boat was at length got off. In a short time the ice began to get thinner, and we got on very well.

The shores of the river, wherever they have been gaining a little, as at the slack part of the bends, are fringed with a dense growth of cottonwood of age and height corresponding with the age of the deposit; the heavy trunks and limbs of the ancient forest towering above them in the background. Some of the newer islands are covered, almost entirely, with cottonwood, the trees decreasing towards the shores, till they become merely switches. The cottonwood, when young, very much resembles Italian poplar.

I here saw, for the first time, the bald-headed, or rather whiteheaded, eagle; two or three of these birds being collected, with a number of Turkey buzzards, about some carrion on the shore of the river.

The towns on this part of the Mississippi are few, and very small, mostly consisting of a store and a few houses. There is great difficulty in getting sites for towns, and advantage is always taken of some rocky, or otherwise durable highland; the treacherous nature of the flats or bottoms, from their liability to the encroachments of the river, rendering it unsafe to build there.

The river now became narrow, with bluffs consisting, in some places, of one continued mass of limestone of between two and three hundred feet high. At one place, where the bluffs are nearly perpendicular on both sides, there remain in the river two huge masses of rock, one of which reminded me of the rock on which Dunbarton Castle stands; it is called Grand Tower.—It is reported that an old soldier, whose daughter had died on one of the boats, selected the top of this rock for a burying place.

A short way above this, and near the mouth of the Kaskaskia, or Okau river, is the town of Chester, in Illinois, where the Mississippi is said to be narrower than at any place between that and New Orleans, a distance of 1,137 miles. A measurement was taken in 1837, when the river was frozen over, and the width was found to be 840 yards. The appearance of the water indicates great depth.

We at length arrived at the landing to which we had been directing our course, and certainly never dreamed that any place

so utterly insignificant could have sent its name so far over the
world.   I never for a moment doubted that there would be, at
least, a few houses and an inn at the landing of a place so old as
Kaskaskia ; but there was not even a tavern of the most wretched
description.   The boat was run in against the bank, a plank run
out, our luggage tumbled ashore, the order given to go on, and
here my companion and I were left ; the sun was just sinking
over the woods of Missouri, and darkness coming on apace.—
After clambering along the broken and muddy edge of the river,
till plastered almost up to the knees, I succeeded in getting up
the precipitous clay bank to level ground, when I saw two young
men standing at no great distance, beside a roofless hut.   I made
my way through a complete smash of huge logs, broken limbs
and brush, and, after accosting the elder of the two, enquired if
I could have my luggage conveyed to Kaskaskia.   He engaged
to take it, and set about getting two horses put to a small waggon.
Whilst this was doing, I stepped into the roofless hut to warm
myself at the fire.   After some conversation with a woman and a
boy, I found they were a family going from Peoria, in Illinois, to
Missouri, and that not having been able to get across the Mississippi on account of the ice, they had taken up their quarters
in this deserted hovel.   The woman had a dreadful cold, and
looked very wretched.   In a few minutes the horses were hitched
to, and away we drove along a very rough track, just as night
had set in.   There is very short space between sundown and
dark in these latitudes, and we had not proceeded a quarter of
a mile till it was dark as midnight, and nothing to be seen
except the huge limbs of the trees between us and the clear
frosty sky.   We soon got out of the woods, and entered on the
extensive clearing which surrounds Kaskaskia, and saw the lights
of that place in the distance, and on arriving, after some delay
occasioned by driving up and down this scattered place in the
dark, our driver being a stranger, we succeeded in reaching the
hotel.

   Kaskaskia, the seat of justice for Randolph county, although
one of the oldest towns in the west, has ceased to be of much
importance, and seems to be in a state of decay.   It was settled
by the French about 1685, and was the capital of the district so
long as that people continued in possession of the country.   The
town is built on an isthmus of about three miles wide, formed by
the Mississippi and Kaskaskia rivers, and is situated on the
right bank of the latter, about seven miles above its embochure.
There is a court house, a Roman catholic church, a nunnery,
and a land-office for the sale of public lands.   The population is

said once to have been seven thousand, but is now about one thousand, and is largely mixed with half-breed French, a race of people remarkable for little besides indolence. The situation of Kaskaskia is very beautiful. The peninsula between the town and the junction of the rivers, constitutes the lower extremity of the famous American Bottom, which is upwards of 80 miles long, and is said to comprise an area of 450 square miles. There is a herd of wild horses on the peninsula, which are considered the property of the town; numbers of them are caught, and broken, and, though not handsome, they are said to be most durable.

I was not a little amused to see hanging, in the bar-room of the hotel, a splendid plan of an extensive city of the name of Downingville, with churches, public buildings, squares, &c., complete, and which, on enquiry, I found was no other than an imaginary city at that wretched place, Kaskaskia landing. This is one of the schemes of the speculator in town lots.

People in this country go early to bed and rise early, the breakfast hour being eight o'clock, when a bell is rung, and all who may happen to be at the hotel at the time must attend, or run the risk of losing their breakfast; it is the same with other meals, dinner being about twelve, and supper (as it is termed) about five o'clock. There is, mostly, great abundance of food on the table, and, in the west, coffee of execrable quality is generally met with at all meals; a lady of the establishment pours it out at a side table, and waiters hand it to the guests. Coffee and tea are, not unfrequently, presented without either sugar or cream. Tea is not much used, and when met with, is almost invariably hyson of indifferent quality.

We remained two nights at Kaskaskia. The second night, on going up stairs to bed, we found a company, consisting of the landlord, a judge of the county, a surveyor, and two or three of the boarders, in the bedroom, playing cards. Money changed hands rapidly in a game somewhat like brag. After looking on for some time, and seeing no likelihood of the company breaking up, we went to bed and fell asleep amid the noise and conversation common on such occasions. Just before I dropt asleep my half-conscious eye caught a vision of the judge tumbling into bed with his clothes on.

Next morning, we got a waggon to take us and our luggage to Plum Prairie, about 18 miles east of Kaskaskia. We crossed the Kaskaskia, or Okau, as it is here termed, by a ferry, on a brilliant December morning. The amphitheatre of woods and bluffs, in which the town is embosomed, though in its winter

F

garb, looked magnificent. The towering, ancient bluffs of the Mississippi, laved by the placid Okau, and in some parts precipitous, in others clothed with a rich profusion of forest trees and underwood, bounded the view to the east; all other points were bounded by the lofty dark forest, whilst a few clumps and scattered trees gave a park-like appearance to the scene. A number of beautiful blue jays were flitting about. There was not a cloud nor a breath of air.

After a hard pull up the bluff, which may be about 300 feet high, we had some glimpses over a great extent of country clad with forest, and apparently lower than our point of view; but I afterwards noticed that the country does frequently fall away from the back of the bluffs, for a considerable distance into the interior. Proceeding on a track through the woods, for a distance of 10 miles, we at length became aware that we were approaching the prairie, and having passed two or three openings of small size, entered on one, which, though not of great extent, possessed the characteristics of that peculiar feature of the west. Almost all the descriptions that I have seen fail to convey to a European any accurate idea of the prairie. In England, the term is rendered meadow, and is applied to a particular kind of grass land; but in America, the term is applied to land of every quality and situation, if naturally denuded of trees. Meadow, in Britain, is, likewise, associated with a verdant, close-grassed turf, which completely hides the soil, even when cropped by cattle; whereas the prairie, if naturally bare, has a sterile appearance, and the richest of it, which mostly carries a rank vegetation of grass or weeds, never at any time appears turfy, or, to use a Scotch word more expressive than any English one I know, *baitle*. Where the prairie has been burnt in the fall, the first appearance of the grass in spring is exceedingly like the braird of wheat. The prairie grasses are few in number, and deep rooted, a circumstance which secures them from being destroyed by the annual conflagrations, and, though coarse, they fatten cattle and horses in a very short time. This, no doubt, may in some measure proceed from the unlimited range affording a constant supply of untouched vegetation. Prairie does not bear much eating, and in the neighbourhood of settlements, where a considerable number of cattle is kept, becomes, to use a common expression, " eat out," when, if the land is rich, a few grasses, differing in kind from those previously grown, with an enormous quantity of weeds, spring up; when poor lands are *eat out*, they become nearly bare. The grasses continue green till frost in the fall, when they die quite down to the earth, affording not the slightest symptom of vegetation till spring. On the untouched prairies, the grass grows to a height of three or four feet, mixed, on the rich flats, with weeds, which sometimes usurp nearly the whole surface, and are so tall that an army of men on horseback might easily be concealed amongst them. Much has been said of the flowers "of every scent and hue" on the prairie, but I must say, that although I saw plenty of weeds, I saw very few flowers of great beauty, and whilst yellow is the prevailing *hue*, the word *scent*, if it mean anything fine, must be taken as a poetical license.

Illinois is free of anything deserving the name of hills; there are, however, very considerable inequalities, occasioned by the cutting down of the watercourses, and the surface of the prairie is frequently what is termed rolling, displaying a succession of easy swells, which at a short distance assume the appearance of an even surface, and the stranger is often startled by the appearance of a herd of cattle or horses, as it were, rising out of the earth, or quietly grazing, where a minute before his eye had wandered over the unvaried ocean of grass.

Prairie consists of almost every variety of soil, from a rich impalpable loam to sterile gravel or sand; I believe there is little of the latter description in Illinois. The rolling is generally the best; that feature evidently being the cause of the superiority, as it facilitates the drainage of the surface of the country, and induces a more abundant growth and deposit of vegetable matter. The flat prairie is apt to be wet, or, as the natives term it, *slashy*, if not connected with some watercourse, by which the water may escape, on the subsidence of the spring freshets; and on being suddenly dried by the sun, at the commencement of summer, is so hardened as to produce little grass, and on that account, is less liable to be run over by the annual fires, and is deprived of the rich black deposit which, there can be no doubt, is the result of these visitations. As a general rule, the higher the prairie is, the better is the soil.

Prairies are to be met with of all sizes, from a few acres, to twelve miles across, and the traveller, on entering some of the larger ones, sees in some directions the forest, a dark line along the verge of the horizon, whilst in others the view is bounded only by the powers of vision. I have heard some estimated at fifty miles long. A large extent of the surface of Illinois consists of prairie, interrupted at intervals by the stripes of timber, which are found almost invariably to accompany the watercourses. These stripes, however, do not by any means follow the windings of the rivers with undeviating accuracy as regards width; on the contrary, they shoot out extensive groves and spurs, varying and greatly adding to the beauty of the landscape. Generally speaking, where watercourses are frequent, the forest prevails; and the large prairies indicate districts removed from the effects of moisture.

It is, perhaps, unnecessary in a work like this, even if I possessed the requisite qualifications, to enter into the subject of the formation of the prairies. I may state, however, that those in the southern part of Illinois appeared to me to have been produced by a deposit, which had been made in comparatively tranquil water, as it consists of very fine calcareous clay, in some places mixed with sand and gravel, the latter mostly about the size of peas or small beans. I never saw a stone on the surface, although I have seen a few of considerable size in the channels of the creeks and branches, and which did not belong to the neighbourhood. The uniformity in the level of the most elevated parts, except in some solitary instances, which, from their peculiar formation, appear to have been islands, may surely be esteemed of some weight, in the presumption that the country has at one time formed the bottom of a lake. It may be asked, why there are such inequalities in its surface—why it is not a dead level, if it formed the bottom of a lake? Many of the inequalities have evidently been caused by the watercourses, and who shall say how, and where the waters ran, before they succeeded in scooping out the present vallies? They might meander and change their courses over the entire surface of what would constitute a muddy plain, and scoop out a number of temporary channels, which, as the level was lowered, would gradually be abandoned for one course. From the general appearance of the country, I think it not at all unlikely that the basin of the lake had been nearly filled up by the immense quantity of matter brought down by the waters at present constituting the Missouri and Mississippi.

The Niagara, or dam of this supposed lake, or body of lakes, seems to have been at Grand Tower (six or seven miles above the mouth of Big Muddy river), where the Mississippi is confined between very high rocks, in many places perpendicular.— Now, looking at Colton and Company's map of Illinois, in which the prairies are accurately indicated, it will be seen that the Grand Tower is their southern limit. When the country is so level that a rise of ten feet on the Mississippi dams back the Okau upwards of twenty miles, it may be readily conceived that an elevation of some hundreds of feet would inundate an immense tract of country.

The barrier at Grand Tower certain̄⬛⬛t account for all
the very extensive prairies in the Miss⬛⬛⬛ley, but it may
perhaps account for those in its more i⬛⬛neighbourhood,
since it might still retain a large body ⬛⬛ after the surface
of the North American continent had e⬛⬛ from the state of
inundation to which it has evidently been very generally exposed.

The question of the prairies having no timber upon them, is,
I think, nearly set at rest, if we allow that they had formed the
bottom of a lake or lakes, whose waters were somewhat suddenly
drained away. The exposed surface would be the depository of
a variety of winged seeds of weeds and grass, and it is natural to
suppose that a rank vegetation of such products would ensue
long before the heavier seeds of trees had advanced any considerable distance. It is not necessary to suppose that man
existed at the period alluded to, in order to account for the
periodical fires, for I have heard it affirmed by people of veracity,
that, independently of human agency, the prairie is frequently set
on fire by lightning; and when we know that hay and straw are
readily set on fire by that fluid, we may admit that a thick crop
of prairie grass, rendered almost as susceptible as tinder by the
clear dry autumn of the climate, may be ignite⬛⬛ the same
means.*

* There is not sufficient proof that the country was inh⬛⬛ the
the deposition of alluvion constituting the present surface. ⬛⬛ ion,
however, that Mr. Caleb Attwood states that he is "credibly ⬛⬛ that
in digging a well at Cincinnati, in this state (Ohio), an arrow h⬛⬛ ound
more than ninety feet below the surface. At Pickaway Plain⬛⬛ whilst several persons were digging a well, several years since, a human skeleton was
found seventeen feet six inches below the surface. This skeleton was seen
by several persons, and among others, by Dr. Daniel Turney, an eminent
surgeon: they all concurred in the belief that it belonged to a human being.
Pickaway Plains are, or rather were, a large prairie, before the land was improved by its present inhabitants. This tract is alluvial to a great depth;
greater probably, than the earth has ever been perforated, certainly than it
ever has been by the hand of man. The surface of the plain is at least one
hundred feet above the highest freshet of the Scioto river near which it lies.
On the surface is a black vegetable mould from three to six and nine feet in
depth; then we find pebbles and shells imbedded among them: the pebbles
are evidently rounded and smoothed by attrition in water, exactly such as
we now see at the bottom of rivers, ponds, and lakes.

"I have examined the spot where this skeleton was found, and am per-
suaded that it was not deposited there by the hand of man, for there are no
marks of any grave, or of any of the works of man; but the earth and pebbles appear to lie in the very position in which they were deposited by the
water. On the north side of a small stream, called Hargus Creek, which at
this place empties itself into the Scioto, in digging through a hill composed
of such pebbles as I have described in Pickaway Plains, at least nine feet
below the surface, several human skeletons were discovered, perfect in every
limb. These skeletons were promiscuously scattered about, and parts of
skeletons were sometimes found at different depths below the surface. This
hill is at least fifty feet above the highest freshets in the Scioto, and is a very
ancient alluvion, where every stratum of sand, clay, and pebbles has been
deposited by the waters of some stream. Other skulls have been taken out

That the annual ⬛⬛⬛⬛rations have prevented the growth of timber on the prairies, is clearly proved by the very vigorous growth of young wood which takes place along their margin, wherever the fire has been kept out for a few years, and in this country, where vegetation proceeds with a rapidity quite astonishing to the native of Britain, many kinds of trees, at the age of three or four years, have attained a height of from eight to twelve feet. Fire will pass through among trees of even smaller dimensions than these without killing, although it materially injures them, and on the ridges and in the groves, which, from their situation, must have been frequently exposed to fire, the old timber is almost invariably unsound, and much of it hollow.

Where the country is becoming settled, the inhabitants generally are opposed to " setting out fire," the risk to houses, crops, and fences being often very great, and a man may see the hard labour of years rendered nugatory in a few hours; besides, the ground is rendered perfectly bare, a great disadvantage to cattle, as they must, of necessity, lie on the frozen ground through winter, and be deprived of any benefit which might have resulted from the de⬛⬛ed grass as fodder—no great benefit, no doubt, but still b⬛⬛ ⬛han none whatever.

In s⬛⬛⬛al enactments against the practice, the burning of the ⬛⬛⬛ either by human agency or by that of lightning, still continues, and is likely to do so, till the country becomes thickly settled, and the prairies so much eat out as to set the incendiary at defiance.

When a farm is new, or surrounded by ground susceptible of ignition, the owner sometimes encircles it with a ring, formed by drawing a few furrows with a plough, which mostly checks the progress of the flames. If this has not been done, and fire is seen approaching, the grass is ignited close to the house and fences, and is allowed to spread, only in a direction leading from them. This " setting out fire to meet fire," as it is termed, may appear, at first sight, a somewhat hazardous experiment, but is not so in reality; and I have seen it practised with perfect success. A person, with a handful of ignited grass, runs along,

of the same hill by persons who, in order to make a road through it, were engaged in taking it away. These bones are very similar to those found in our mounds, and probably belonged to the same race of men; a people short and thick, not exceeding generally five feet in height, and, very possibly, they were not more than four feet six inches. . . . Fragments of antique pottery, and even entire pots, of coarse earthenware, have been found likewise in the excavations of the Illinois salt-works, at the depth of eighty feet and more from the surface. . . . This fossil pottery is stated not to differ materially from that which frequently occurs in the mounds supposed to have been formed by the aboriginal Indians."

shaking it so as to disengage some particles of the flaming materials, which fall among and instantly set fire to the standing grass. After having proceeded in this manner for fifteen or twenty yards, he returns, and with a branch beats out, on the side next to the fence, &c., the fire which has begun, of course, to spread in opposite directions, and this operation is repeated, till he has performed the circuit of his location, or secured it from danger. It is by no means safe, however, to trust to this method, if the line of fence is very extensive, as the fire sometimes comes up so unexpectedly, and at such a pace, that there is no time left for doing anything to check its progress. I have seen it stated, that a man on horseback has no chance of escaping by speed from prairie fire, but confess I never saw it attain any such speed as to warrant the assertion, although it may sometimes travel three or four miles an hour. Still, at the season of the annual conflagrations, the traveller may run some risk, as from the thick state of the atmosphere, he may, before he is aware, march right up to an approaching line of some miles in length, when, if he have not the means of raising fire, or be on foot and without some friendly creek, at no great distance, to fly to, it may require considerable self-possession and exertion to escape a horrible death. But if he can raise fire, and set it out before his enemy come up to him, he has a bared spot to stand upon, and, like the enchanter in his circle, sets the raging fiend at defiance. So effectually does the fire do its work, that the earth is left quite bare, and a person may walk upon it without sustaining any injury, immediately after the fire has passed.

Few sights can be grander than that of a prairie on fire during the night; the huge body of flame spread far and wide, leaping and plunging like the waves of the sea in a gale against a rocky coast, and emitting a continued roar like that of a heavy surf when heard from a short distance. The whole country is lighted up for miles, and the sky (where not obscured by volumes of smoke) is like a sheet of red hot metal. But the scene is by far the grandest when the fire is in the woods, particularly if they have been preserved from its ravages for some seasons, as there is then a dense growth of young trees, mostly of kinds retaining their withered leaves, mixed with grass and weeds. Owing to the covering of the branches above, a draft is engendered which drives the flames up among the limbs of the tall forest,* yet so

---

* I passed through a grove in which the fire had been the previous day, and saw a huge trunk, hollow and without the top, into which the fire had got by a hole at the root, and was roaring up through the cavity like the blast of a smelting furnace, and darting far into the air.

rapid is the course of the fire, that none of the large trees are seized by it, except such as are dead or decayed, and these are left like pillars of fire, some of them continuing to burn for days, a loud crash at intervals intimating their downfall.

There is every reason to believe that coal prevails throughout a large proportion of the Mississippi Valley, though, owing to the abundance of wood, the inhabitants have not hitherto paid much attention to that mineral.   A great drawback on the usefulness of the coal seams on the prairies is their frequently having no cover beyond the alluvial deposits of gravel and clay, which, when deep, render the coals quite unattainable by ordinary means.   In some places the seams are so near the surface, that they are cut into by the waggon wheels in wet weather.— The seams are sometimes three or four feet thick.   The coal is bituminous, and of excellent quality.

CHAPTER III.

Whilst the population on the great rivers and other thorough-fares is of a very mixed and doubtful character, much of that on the prairies and purely agricultural districts consists of decent people of simple manners, and is as unlike that of the eastern states as if they were of different nations. In the west, the Yankee is not very generally nor highly esteemed, as he is considered "too quirky." If any one has been cheated, he is said to have been "yankeed;" and any worthless thing, which is tin-selled and varnished, is said to be "yankeed over." The population of Randolph county, as in the states generally, has been derived from many parts of the world. There are Dutch, Germans, Swiss, Yankees, Irish, Scotch, a few English, and a number from the more southern states; the latter, as I understood, having immigrated to this part of the country, owing to the dislike they had to slavery. They are, at all events, very generally abolitionists. Another reason might be their want of means to become slaveholders, a man's respectability being, in a great measure, proportioned to the number of slaves in his possession. However this may be, I found many of these men intelligent, and of good moral character, and generally professing a religious creed, less whimsical than some others among a very motley class of Christians. There is a congregation of old light Cameronians, and one of, I think, Anti-burghers, with resident pastors, at Sparta, (late Columbus), near Flat Prairie, in this county, and a Roman Catholic Church and Nunnery at Kaskaskia. There are also circuit preachers sent out by the heads of different persuasions, who make regular visits to different parts of the country, and who are partly remunerated by the subscriptions of a portion of the community. For the religion of the state generally, I shall quote a few particulars from "Illinois in 1837," a work published by S. Augustus Mitchell, Philadelphia:—

"The Methodist Episcopal Church is the most numerous.—

H

The Illin   ference, which embraces this state and a portion
of Wiscon   ritory, in 1835 had 61 circuit preachers, 308
local preachers, and 15,097 members of society.   They sustain
preaching in every county, and in a large number of the settlements.

"The Baptist denomination includes 22 associations, 260
churches, 160 preachers, and 7,350 communicants.

"The Presbyterians have one synod, eight presbyteries, and
about 80 churches, 60 ministers, and 2,500 members.

"There are 12 or 15 Congregationalist churches united in an
association, and several ministers.

"The Methodist Protestant denomination has one conference,
22 ministers, and 344 members.

"The Reformers, as they term themselves, or 'Campbellites,'
as others call them, have several large, and a number of small
societies, a number of preachers, and several hundred members,
including the *Christian* body with which they are in union.—
They immerse all who profess to believe in Christ for the remis-
sion of sins, but differ widely from orthodox Baptists on some
points of doctrine.

"The Cumberland Presbyterians have two or three presbyteries, twelve or fifteen preachers, and several hundred communicants.

"There are two churches of Reformed Presbyterians, or Cove-
nanters, one minister, and about 280 communicants, with a few
families scattered in other parts of the state.   There are also
two or three societies of Associate Reformed Presbyterians or
Seceders.

"In McLean county is a society of United Brethren, or, as
some call them, Dutch Methodists.

"The Dunkards have five or six societies, and some preachers
in this state.

"There are several Lutheran congregations, with preachers.

"The Protestant Episcopal church has an organized diocese,
eight or ten congregations, and seven or eight ministers.

"There are small societies of Friends, or Quakers, in Tazewell
and Crawford counties; and a few Mormons, scattered through
the state.

"The Roman Catholics are not numerous.   They have a dozen
congregations, eight or ten priests, and a population between
five and six thousand, including old and young.   A convent and
boarding-school for young ladies is in operation at Kaskaskia.
The Roman Catholics are mostly about the old French villages
and the labourers along the line of canal.

"There is considerable expression of good feeling amongst

the different religious denominations, and the members frequently hear the preachers of each other, as there are but few congregations that are supplied every Sabbath. The qualifications of the clergymen are various. A number of them are men of talents, learning, influence, and unblemished piety. Others have had but few advantages in acquiring either literary or theological information, and yet are good speakers and useful men.

" In general, there are as many professors of religion, of some description, in proportion to the population, as in most of the states. The number will not vary far from 40,000, or one to ten."

There is a good deal of superstition, belief in witchcraft, omens, lucky times, &c., particularly amongst the hunters, who are the pioneer settlers of America, and of whom very many can neither read nor write. I have heard singular stories of rifles being witched, and anything very singular in nature is ascribed to the devil, as "devil's oven," "devil's lettuce," "devil's mare" (the last a singularly shaped insect) ; a species of superstition which seems in some shape to have infected the darker stages in the progress of every people. I was so unlucky as to afford what was considered an incontestable proof of the truth of witchcraft.

I had strolled into the woods with my rifle to look out for a buck. It was summer and near sundown, that and early morning being the only times, at this season, when deer are to be seen afoot, as they lie hid through the day. I had not been long out, when I thought I saw, among some hazels, about a quarter of a mile off, some part of the body of a deer, which in the summer months has a coat in colour somewhat like that of a light red cow. I made a detour, in order to take advantage of the cover of some bushes and trees, and after a good deal of crawling on all fours, and sometimes at full length, got within about eighty yards of the spot On looking past a tree, behind which I was lying, I saw two deer standing, evidently listening and ready to bound off. Having lain motionless for some time, to regain my wind and reassure them, I cautiously pushed forward my rifle, and having taken deliberate aim, fired at the one nearest me, which fell, as I thought, plump down on the spot. On raising myself up a little, I saw what I conceived to be the head of the deer above the long grass, and fearing it might escape me, lay still and reloaded.— On looking past the tree again, I saw not only the head still in the same place, but the other deer also. One deer was quite enough in such hot weather, but this fellow was standing so

beautifully that I was tempted, and fired at him. I heard the
bullet play thump on his ribs, and off he bounded. No doubt I
had not got the powder properly down the barrel when I lay and
loaded behind the tree. Well, well, let him go, thought I, one
is quite enough. On looking towards the spot, I still saw the
deer's head, though not quite so distinctly, as it seemed to have
settled down among the grass. This was a good sign, so I loaded
again, and marched up, when—there was no deer—no blood—
not even the slightest trail in the grass ! After looking round
for a few moments, I went back to the tree from which I had
fired, and could see nothing at all like either a deer or a deer's
head.

I repeat that such superstitions as I have mentioned are
mostly confined to the hunters and early settlers. It may easily
be supposed that the character of such a mixed population
exhibits no near approach to individuality.

Not long after arriving at our destination, we were invited,
amongst others of the family with which we resided, to a corn
shocking or husking frolic. The person who intends to have a
frolic, or *bee*, rides round among his neighbours a few days
before and invites them to attend, and the invitation is very
generally complied with.

On the present occasion, three of us started through a grove
of about a mile in width, which intervened between us and the
place of our destination. It was a beautiful, clear morning in
January, and although there had been a pretty sharp frost
through the night, was exceedingly mild, being tempered by the
rays of an unclouded sun. Our route, though mostly wooded,
was at intervals varied by openings displaying fine swelling
knolls or knobs, as they are called, clothed with hazels, whilst
the intervening vallies of prairie, swept gently round their
bases. Here and there were clumps of oaks and hiccory, and
single trees almost overtopped and festooned with vines, telling
of rare beauty and shade in the summer heats. At one point,
we had a view of the prairie stretching away in the distance,
dotted here and there with a cabin shooting its pale blue smoke
into the still air, the far woods lining the distant horizon like a
bank of clouds.

For some time before we arrived, we heard ringing throug-
the woods the fitful sounds of voices, which became more cont
tinuous till we at once emerged from the grove, and arrived a
the scene of action, which was situated on the margin of the
prairie. It was a scene full of novelty. Groups of wild-looking
men, with long hair spread over their shoulders, and clad in

homespun coats, and trowsers of Dutch build, were standing about, laughing and talking, whilst all around were seen fancifully caparisoned horses, with long tails and manes, attached by the bridles to the pliant branches of the trees. New comers were pouring in from all quarters, some carrying long rifles on their shoulders, and accoutred in belt and bullet pouch.

In the house was a long table groaning under piles of eatables for those who had come far, or felt inclined to partake of them.

In a short time we proceeded to the corn cribs, one of which had been unroofed, the more readily to receive the husked corn, whilst the walls of that in which the corn was lying, had been almost entirely removed; the roof and logs constituting one end of it, having been taken away, whilst the logs forming the side walls had their disengaged extremities swayed outwards, so that the heap could be surrounded on three sides.

All things being prepared, a noisy consultation was held, when it was resolved and carried that the heap should be divided into two equal parts. On this being done, two men were pitched upon as captains of the heaps, who having called sides, the battle commenced.

No match at football or shinty was ever engaged in with more uproarious animation. The yells of defiance, mingled with whoops and shrieks in Indian style, arose in one continued medley, and reverberated far through the woods, whilst an unceasing shower of corn streamed through the air towards the roofless crib, many of the ears flying wide of the mark, and one now and then making a dubiously tangential movement, which brought it into contact with the body of some unlucky wight. Shortly after the commencement, there were some new arrivals, towards whom the tide of vociferation was directed. " Come along, Andy—go ahead—whoop, here's the major—halloo, major, graze it—well done, *Kurnel*—look at him—see how he cuts gravel—whoop, halloo, &c."

As the proprietor of the corn was a temperance man, there was no whisky allowed. On similar occasions, however, where the master of the ceremonies is less strict, there is a plentiful libation of that most execrable of spirits, corn whisky, or of peach brandy. A red ear, which is now and then met with among white flint corn, is always a signal for a round of the bottle.

After the husking was over, as many of the company as could gain admittance at one time, entered the house to partake of the multitude of viands which covered the table. As this is an

I

occasion on which the *old woman*, as a wife, of whatever age, is familiarly termed, makes a display, no trouble is spared, and she, with some of her neighbours, labours for a day or two beforehand with a most praiseworthy and successful zeal, to twist each article in the larder into the most various and recondite shapes possible.

Some travellers very kindly give us a list of the bills of fare; but I cannot, I am sorry to say, gratify the reader by so doing, nor would he, perhaps, be much the wiser were I to inform him that there were Johnny cake and hoe cake, pona bread and dodger, salt bread and milk bread, pumpkin and other pies, with a number of fantastic freaks in pastry, that belong to no kindred or nation; suffice it to say, that among many examples of ingenuity, there was abundance of really good and substantial fare, accompanied by the never-failing coffee. After all had partaken of the good things, and had lounged about the door for some time, to talk over the news of the day, the company dropt away, each taking the route for home.

Sometimes, on similar occasions, a number of the ladies of the neighbourhood assemble, and the affair finishes off with amusements, and if a fiddler can be procured, with a dance.

From Christmas to the middle of January is the time for killing the hogs for market, and for home use through the season, and pork being a staple commodity in the economy of an American household, every farmer has a herd of these animals. At all seasons, except when put up to get corn, to feed them off and firm their flesh, which is soft and oily when merely mast fed, they roam at large through the woods, with little trouble to the owner beyond that of bringing them home now and then, and giving them a little corn to prevent them from running wild, or wandering to a distant range. Those newly littered must also be searched for, in order that they may be preserved from the attack of the wolf.

There is, perhaps, no animal which the western farmer possesses, reared with so little trouble and expense, and which, at the same time, adds so largely to his comforts, as the hog. At all times, except during the short winter, when the earth is bound up by frost, he roams at large, at some seasons rooting in the woods and prairies, at others luxuriating amidst a great abundance of mast, consisting of acorns, hiccory nuts, walnuts, hazel nuts, &c.; and the pork fed in this way, though soft and apt to run much to grease in the cooking, is the sweetest I ever tasted.

A hog killing is one of the great affairs, and such individuals as are accounted dexterous at the operation are in request at killing time. The hogs being very wild and savage, any uproar or squealing makes them so outrageous, that they become quite unmanageable. A rifle is mostly used to bring them down, the marksman doing his best to kill them dead on the spot, by shooting them through the head. After every precaution to prevent such an occurrence has been used, they sometimes break through the fence, and run off to the woods, squandering in all directions. When this takes place, the owner and his assistants hunt them like deer, and shoot them wherever they can find them, without being very nice in taking aim at any particular part of the body.

I happened to be invited to a hog-killing, and on arriving, with two others, at the place, found that the condemned grunters had broken loose from their pen, though luckily they had got into a large field of fifty or sixty acres, surrounded by a good rail fence. This was the first time they had broken fence, and the man accounted for their doing so by saying, "they had a mighty great notion of what was going to take place, as he had been oftener to them that morning than he used to, and had made them mad by laying some more rails on the fence of the pen." The affair was not quite so bad as if they had taken to the woods, still, no energetic measures could be used, as even a good rail fence is a trifle opposed to an enraged hog. Most unluckily, there was only one gun, and that an old smooth bore, which might have done well enough at the pen, but which made very random work at a long distance. However it would not do to stand and talk, as the thermometer was down very near zero, and a northwester beginning to sweep the prairie, so to work one of the party set with the old gun, whilst the rest, by walking on the opposite side of the field, kept the hogs as near him as possible. After crouching about for some time, the marksman fired and brought down one, which was immediately bled by a man who followed closely for that purpose. A considerable time elapsed before a shot was got at another, standing, as it did, at some distance. The shot took effect in the animal's body, and over he tumbled, but quickly regaining his feet, set off floundering and squealing. The old fellow threw down his gun, and scrambled over the fence, and, accompanied by his henchman with the knife and a stout dog, pursued across the field full split. The field was ploughed, hard frozen, and covered with loose snow, a conjunction of circumstances most unfavourable to speedy progress; and the poor hog and his pursuers were seldom all afoot at the same time, and when the dog

got up, and a series of short cuts and turns took place, the affair became almost a scramble on all fours.   There was much
need for despatch, however, for the cries of their wounded companion having aroused the rest of the herd, they came up with
erect bristles and open mouth to the rescue.   The hog was
seized and stabbed, just in the nick of time, and the men, with
some difficulty, made good their retreat; not so the dog, which,
being fierce and unwilling to quit his victim, had the back part
of his head laid open for his temerity.   After considerable delay
and a series of operations somewhat similar to those described,
the whole were slaughtered and hauled up on a sled to the house,
where preparations had been made for scalding them.   This
process took place out of doors.   A couple of logs of about
eighteen inches diameter were rolled nigh together, a proper
supply of lighted fuel was put between them, and over it were
placed all the pots and kettles that could be mustered about the
place.   The water, when boiling, was poured into a barrel with
one of its ends out, which was placed in an inclined position, and
into which the hogs were soused over head and ears.

The northwester had become a stiffish breeze, and the day
was dreadfully cold—so cold, indeed, that the tops of the bristles became frozen together in a few seconds after the hogs were
withdrawn from the hot water, and the carcases were as hard as
wood in not very many hours.

The breed of hogs in this part of the country is very bad;
they are long-nosed, thin creatures, with legs like greyhounds;
and, like the greyhound among dogs, seem to be the kind formed
for speed and agility among swine, as they think nothing of galloping a mile at a heat, or of clearing fences which a more civilized hog would never attempt.   Still, as the hog of a pioneer
settler has, at some seasons, need for all the activity he can exert to
procure a subsistence, he may after all be the best fitted for the
backwoods.

Till about the middle of January the weather was very fine,
with moderately frosty nights and clear sunshiny days; but
about that time winter commenced in earnest, and the north-
west winds, with a temperature at zero, swept the prairie with a
chilling blast, that made the bones of one's face ache.   The trees
might be heard through the night cracking from the effects of
the frost.   Though the woods felt very cold, yet from the comparative stillness of the air in their recesses, they were never to
compare to the prairie, whose keen blast seemed to penetrate
the very bones.   A dead calm and a gale respectively at zero,
are two very different affairs; the former being quite tolerable

with moderate exercise, whilst the latter is all but insufferable, unless one be wrapped up like a pack, and have nothing exposed but the nose and eyes.

The very severe cold lasted only a few days, during which time nobody seemed inclined to stir far from the fire; and roarers we kept. The chimney and chimney-brace were generally on fire several times through the day, but we had some water ready, standing in a bucket, close to the fire, to keep it from freezing. The house was so open, that whilst we were sitting as near to the fire as we could for burning our clothes, our backs were starving from the current of air generated by the heat. Most unfortunately, our luggage had not come along, and we had no books, except two or three, in the house, among which were the Confession of Faith and Burns' Poems; which were read and re-read from beginning to end, with a zeal, as regards the former, that would have been exemplary had there been greater choice. I attempted to write, but, although I heated the ink, which was hard frozen, and sat within as short distance of the fire as could, with the paper on my knee, I could not write one word I the ink seemed to vanish up the pen, and was frozen in an instant.

Prairie hens (pinnated grouse) and quails came about the fences in hundreds, and with a very primitive trap, made of split sticks, with a figure 4 trigger, we caught numbers of both within view of the door of the house. Owing to the carelessness of a forwarding agent, a Mr Redman, at Shawneetown, our luggage, with which were our guns, did not arrive till spring, so that we got no shooting at this time.

Time hung heavily on our hands, and as soon as the weather moderated, I shouldered an axe and went to the woods with the choppers. My coup d'essai was on an old gnarled hiccory, for firewood; and if the *old woman* had had none but me to depend upon, she might have got clear of boiling pot or kettle for that day. By and bye, I became more expert, and eventually could bring down a good large tree with comparative ease, and got initiated into all the mysteries of rail splitting.

Every one has read or heard of the prodigies performed by the American chopper; and the dexterity and speed with which many of them accomplish their work, are really surprising. As with other operations requiring great dexterity, it is necessary to commence chopping when young, a person past middle age very rarely becoming a proficient. But what would the American be without his axe of the true Yankee cut? He would be dexterous, no doubt, in the use of any axe, according to its

K

capabilities; but I very much doubt if he could do the half of the chopping and splitting with any axe I every saw in Britain. The Yankee axe, with its handle, is a scientific implement——much more so, indeed, than many who use it are aware of——and is mostly beautifully made of the very best materials, cast steel of the finest quality being used. Among the best and handsomest I saw were of the brand *Collin's and Co., Hartford,* (Connecticut).*

After a tree has been felled, the workman gets on to it, and by cutting into the middle from opposite sides, detaches a length of ten or eleven feet (the former length is usual in the west, the latter in Canada), the curves on each side being so managed that the end of the detached piece is cut straight across to facilitate the operation of splitting. Iron wedges are introduced at this end, and when an opening has been made, wooden ones are introduced, and the log is halved, quartered, and finally reduced to rails of the desired size.

A chopping *bee,* where twenty or thirty choppers are collected, is an animating affair. The forest resounds with the blows of the axe, and ever and anon some tall monarch of the woods begins to topple, reclines gently to one side, and then rushes, with accelerating speed and the roar of a whirlwind, to the thundering earth, amidst a chaos of smashed limbs and dust.

Accidents sometimes occur, from the descent of pieces of the shattered limbs, which have been pitched into the air; and my friend was one day felled to the earth with one which descended from a height of seventy or eighty feet, and though the touch was so slight, that it barely ruffled the skin of his face, yet some of his teeth were splintered by it.

So soon as the weather becomes mild and settled in spring, ploughing is commenced, to prepare the ground for *corn,* as maize or Indian corn is invariably termed, which is got in about the end of April or beginning of May; past the middle of May being thought too late, although corn planted about the beginning of June is some-

---

* I saw in Canada some axes which had been made in England from a model sent for the purpose. The person who had them told me that, although cheaper than those made in the country, they were by no means so good; in fact, that they were useless. I have often been ashamed to see the worthless trash, in the shape of tools, cutlery, &c., sent out from this country to the United States; but the Americans are tired of this, and now manufacture a large quantity of tools of very superior quality. The fact that a very large proportion of the finest steel manufactured in this country, is exported to America, speaks volumes. The author of " Manufactures in Metal," in Lardner's Cyclopædia, remarks——" It has been said that there is probably ten times as much Hoop L sent to America as is consumed in this country, though the amount of steel used at home is at least fifty times greater than the amount sent to the United States."

times a very good crop. There are several kinds of corn, but the kind almost invariably planted in the district to which I refer, and over a large portion of Illinois, is the white flint, which appears best to suit the climate. It is a grain requiring good soil, and a long course of warm weather, to bring it to maturity. From fifty to eighty bushels an acre is reckoned a good crop on most prairie; but on the Ohio and Mississippi bottoms, 100 and even 120 bushels are sometimes raised—an immense increase, when it is considered that one bushel of corn is quite enough of seed for ten acres.

This grain is the indigent farmer's main dependence, for without it, I do not see how he could live and support his stock. It affords the means of subsistence to every living thing about his place, particularly during periods of snow, or hard frost; for not only is everything, down to the dog and cat, fond of the grain, in some shape or another, but its very stalks, leaves, and husks afford a valuable fodder for cattle and horses. Then, who but must admire the facility with which it is raised; the small amount of labour required; the trifling quantity of seed; and the most abundant return. It is not like other grain easily injured; but once ripe, there it stands, setting at defiance rain, frost, snow, and every vicissitude of climate, often through great part of winter; and when gathered, it is frequently piled into heaps standing on the ends of the stalks in the fields, without any covering, or thrown, often on the bare ground, into a crib but poorly defended from wet, and permeable to the snow and drift. It is to the poor of this country what the potato is to the poor Irish, and can be cooked and turned into as many shapes; and, speaking from my own experience, is equally wholesome, perhaps more so in a hot climate. The white flint is much sweeter and more palatable than the yellow corn, which is the kind mostly imported to England.

The ground being ploughed, is, mostly without any harrowing, scratched with the plough, at distances of four feet apart; and after the field has been gone over in this way, similar scratches or furrows are drawn at right angles to the previous ones, thus forming a series of crossings, four feet apart in all directions. Exactly at the spot where the furrows intersect each other, from three to five grains of corn are dropped, and lightly covered over with a hoe.

When the plants have risen about twelve inches, they are thinned down to four on every hill, and if the seeds have not sprung, more are planted and thinned out afterwards. The ground ought to be gone over with a light one-horse plough, at least two or three times, in order to keep down the weeds, and to expose a fresh surface of soil.

Store, or sod corn, is planted on the breaking up of prairie, the seeds being scattered along every third furrow; and thus the land is ploughed and a crop put in at the same time. A bushel of seed will plant four acres. After this crop is removed from the ground in the fall, and without any farther preparation of the land, wheat, at the rate of one bushel an acre, is sown and harrowed in. Thus with one ploughing and a harrowing are secured two crops, the corn averaging from fifteen to twenty bushels, and the wheat about twenty bushels an acre; the return in both cases, however, depending very much on the style in which the prairie has been broken.

On good land, the corn stalks are often eight or ten, and sometimes from twelve to fifteen feet long, with a seedy-looking tassel at the top, and carrying one or two good ears, at about two-thirds of their height from the ground. If the ears on one stalk exceed two, they are small, and of less value than a single good one. Some of the smaller kinds of corn will, I believe, produce more ears.

When the corn is ripe, which it generally is about the middle of October, or five and a half months from the time it is planted, it is cut down with a large knife, or a piece of an old scythe put into a handle, and is either hauled home, or piled up in the field with the lower end of the stalks standing on the ground. Frequently it is left uncut, the ear alone being pulled and stored in the corn crib till the proper season for a husking frolic. When the stalks are thus left standing, the cattle are turned into the enclosure, to feed an hour or two every day during winter. I have seen corn stand all winter without being gathered, and without suffering any injury from the weather, so well is it protected by its voluminous husk. If left in this state, however, it is destroyed by deer, prairie fowl, field mice, squirrels, &c.

Wheat is raised in considerable quantity, and of excellent quality, frequently weighing upwards of 60lbs. a bushel; a very fair weight when it is considered that the system of dressing is very clumsy and defective. It is generally sown in October, on ground where corn has grown the preceding season; and after oats, castor oil beans, and sometimes on the newly broken prairie. One bushel of seed per acre is quite enough, as every grain seems to grow, and stool or spread out into thick and distinct patches. Perhaps the prairie soil, as it never binds at any season, but is at all times, except when frozen or steeped with recent rains, as friable as ashes, may favour this overspreading of the roots, which certainly very materially detracts from the increase, as each grain produces a close matted plant, from which result slight straw and a small ear. That this is not entirely the effect of climate, is proved by better and more abundant crops of wheat being grown on the timber and ridge lands of the creeks, where the soil consists of a limestone alluvion, without any addition of a purely prairie soil. I am of opinion, that the prairies will grow more abundant crops of wheat than at present, when the prairie soil shall have been worn down; but nothing like the abundance of the wheat crops of our own country must be expected, as it will never be realized either in Illinois or in any hot climate. From twenty to twenty-two bushels per acre, I consider, fully the average of all the wheat I saw in Illinois.

Wheat harvest commences in June, and there is a ready market for as much as can be raised, at a price which had been steadily increasing for some years, till it was affected by the late monetary convulsion (that of 1841-2.)*

Oats are raised in some parts of the state, and yield a plentiful crop; but the climate is too hot and speedy for them, and the grain is imperfectly formed. They make very good feed, however, either when thrashed, or when cut early and seasoned, they are given to cattle, corn and all; the latter, no doubt, being a very improvident plan; but as long as there is no other system of thrashing but that of treading out with horses, it is perhaps the best that can be followed. Two bushels an acre is the quantity generally sown; and the return is frequently above forty bushels.

Uplands rice is sometimes raised, but not in great quantity. I have reason to believe that it succeeds in the southern parts of the state, where I have also seen millet, which looked very well. Buck wheat is frequently grown.

There is seldom any barley planted in Randolph county, but it would appear that it can be raised with advantage. I was informed by a gentleman, on whose word I can place entire confidence, that he had seen sixteen bushels of this grain gathered from a quarter of an acre; but a prejudice exists against it on account of the difficulty and annoyance experienced in dressing it, from the want of proper implements.

The cotton plant is frequently to be seen, but not in any great quantity, as the inhabitants raise it only for their own use. When taken care of, it grows well, and produces very good cotton.

---

* Wheat in Randolph county was in 1830, 50 cents.; in 1837, 1 dollar, 2 cents.; and in 1841, 80 cents. per bushel.

Tobacco may be raised in any quantity.

Potatoes are almost universally planted, and yield a fair return; but are by no means so good as those in Britain.

The sweet potato thrives very well, and is very much esteemed by the natives. It runs some risk from late frosts in spring.

Musk melons, water melons, squashes, pumpkins, gourds, and cucumbers, of excellent quality, are raised in great abundance, by merely dropping a few seeds here and there among the rows of corn. The pumpkins are raised chiefly as feed for horses and cattle, which are very fond of them.

Turnips have several times been tried by a Scotch gentleman from Roxburghshire; but without success. When planted in spring, they are overtaken by the summer drought, and are either scorched or forced to seed. When planted in summer, the ground is so dry, that the seed does not vegetate, unless moistened by a thunder shower, which is so transient in its effects, where the soil is exposed to the sun's rays, that the germs are soon withered; and when planted at the commencement of the fall, although there is still plenty of time between that and winter, their growth is checked by the frosts which invariably occur, with greater or less intensity, through the night. The high value which a British farmer habitually attaches to the turnip, may cause him to regret the failure of this plant on any part of the earth's surface to which he may emigrate, and acting on preconceived opinions, he may throw away both time and money in an unavailing struggle with nature. A change of country is not all that an emigrant must effectuate; he must also make a change, to a great extent, in his habits, both of thought and action—he must adapt himself to circumstances.

I very much doubt if turnips will ever be profitably raised in the southern parts of Illinois; but Indian corn is a very good substitute, and is much more varied in its uses. Large numbers of cattle and hogs are annually fattened on this grain, which seems to answer the purpose much better than any we cultivate in this country. It is very nutritious, and less stimulating, perhaps, than any other grain.*

Although the farmer may fail in raising turnip, I have reason to believe that there is no difficulty in raising beet, or mangel wurzel; and have heard fifty or sixty tons mentioned as the produce of an acre; a quantity which, I believe, exceeds the average in England.

Castor oil beans are raised in considerable quantities; from fifteen to twenty bushels an acre being an average crop. They

* Mush, a sort of porridge made of it, and eaten with milk, is highly spoken of as a light food for dyspeptics.

are planted from the middle to the end of April, and generally begin to ripen about the end of July, when it is necessary to go through the plants every day and cut off the ripe pods, which are deprived of the beans by being exposed to the sun. The beans can be sold very readily, as presses for extracting the oil are in almost every town. A bushel of beans affords about one gallon and a half of oil.

All kinds of grain, except maize, are cut down with the cradle scythe; from two to three acres of oats, and about two of wheat, being accounted a good day's work. When grain is not lodged, this is an excellent method of cutting it, as it is both speedy and efficient. A scythe of between three and four feet is generally used, and is fixed to a sned or handle with a peculiar twist. Four or five fingers, at intervals of five or six inches above one another, extend from the heel to within two or three inches of the point, in the direction, and with nearly the curve, of the blade. The fingers are supported by a rod, inserted into the sned at the heel of the scythe; by another rod that is attached to the back of the scythe by means of a punched hole, about a foot or fourteen inches from the heel; and by braces from the latter rod to the sned. There are as many braces as fingers, with the addition of a brace from the top of the rod inserted at the heel, to the sned. The rod or support at the heel must be placed at such an angle to the sned, as to ensure its being perpendicular to the ground, and of course parallel with standing grain, when the cradle is in the act of being used.

There are two methods of laying down the grain with the cradle, of which the more generally adopted is "swathing"; that is, arranging the cut grain, when delivered from the scythe, in a continuous row, with the stalks at right angles to the course of the mower; the cut ends lying evenly along, near his left foot. By the other method, "griping" as it is termed, the grain, after the stroke is made, is collected on the braces, by turning up the fingers of the scythe, when it is seized by the left hand and dropped upon the ground. Two handfuls are laid together, and constitute a small-sized sheaf.

Hay, in great abundance, may be had on the prairie. The inhabitants say that it is not good, and that cattle do not thrive well on it; but one may surely entertain some doubt of the correctness of this opinion, when the nutritious quality of the grasses is so evident in the speedy fattening of cattle and horses. The fact is, the hay is never made early enough in the season; but, on the contrary, the grass is allowed to stand till it has in a great measure become ripe, and has lost the greater part of its juices. On asking why they did not mow earlier in the season, it was answered that "the grass was so tender, and dried so much away, that it took twice as much labour to get the same quantity early, that it did later in the season; besides, when it was mown late, there was some *bone* in it, and it took some eating; whereas, when it was mown earlier, the cattle *swallowed it by mouthfuls* — there was no such thing as getting them enough;"—arguments which require no comment, and which will be fully appreciated by any practical farmer in this country.

The grass cut down in the forenoon is put up into cocks in the afternoon, and may be carried home in a few days.

Many farmers, who have been some time settled, have timothy meadows, which are regularly mown every season, and which, when they are situated on a moist bottom, yield a most luxuriant crop.

There is a sort of grass, with whose botanical name I am unacquainted, but which, in the States, is called "blue grass," and which, I believe, is extensively planted in some districts. I saw it, in two instances, tried on the prairie; in one, among red clover, on prairie termed second rate, i. e., limestone alluvion, with little black loam upon it, where it appeared to grow very well; in the other, on very fine rich prairie, where it was completely overwhelmed with tall weeds.

Artificial grasses seem to thrive best on the ridge lands, and on the back of the river bluffs, where the soil consists of a fine alluvial clay, uncovered, or at most very slightly so, by the black loam of the prairies. I saw some very fine fields of red clover, quite free from weeds, on such land, in the neighbourhood of St. Louis. Indeed, the ridge lands do not produce weeds to any great extent, either before or after breaking up, and after wheat is cut, the stubbles remain bare through the rest of the summer and autumn. On the prairie, on the contrary, wheat is no sooner cut than the weeds begin to shew themselves, and in a week or two the whole surface is green with a dense crop; which attains a height of three or four feet, and ripens in the fall.

There is a system of introducing artificial grasses into the prairie, which I have sometimes heard mentioned, but of which I cannot speak from my own observation, but shall give an extract from a letter, in which it is referred to by the Hon. H. L. Ellsworth, Superintendent of the Patent-office at Washington :—" There is a practice mentioned by Mr Newell, and highly recommended by others, of putting in hayseed without ploughing the ground; this is done by burning prairie grass in the spring and harrowing in the seed. The seed catches quick and grows well. Blue grass especially succeeds in this way, and the grass will sustain stock all winter without cutting hay or fodder for them. A large drove of horses was kept last winter at Indianapolis on blue grass in the open fields, at the small expense of one dollar per head per month." I may remark that the soil about Indianapolis is not prairie, but a fine limestone loam reclaimed from the forest, and approaching in quality and appearance to the ridge lands above mentioned. There is no doubt that artificial grasses of various sorts might readily be cultivated on such land, but I must say that I am somewhat sceptical with respect to the successful cultivation of such grasses on the prairie proper; by which term I would designate that prairie, whose upper stratum consists of a pure black mould of eight or ten inches deep, and evidently the residuum of burnt vegetable matter; as it is of so loose and friable a nature, that the superficially-rooted grasses, if they could be preserved from being overwhelmed by weeds, could scarcely withstand the summer droughts. It may be said that the annual fires tend to destroy such grasses, which may account for their non-appearance; but I have examined prairie from which fire had been kept for several years, and never could see any such grasses, whilst on ridge land, under similar circumstances, and on the clay thrown up from wells,* I have seen some, and amongst others, the common white clover.

* The plants springing from the clay thrown out of these wells, add another to the numerous proofs of the durability of the germinating principle in seeds. White clover, and some other grasses, never seen on the rich prairie, spring and grow luxuriantly, mixed with heavy-seeded plants and shrubs, of which there are frequently no examples in the immediate neighbourhood. When a portion of the ancient forest has been levelled by a thundergust, it often happens that there succeeds a growth of young wood of kinds entirely distinct from that which previously occupied the soil.

CHAPTER IV.

The ploughs in Illinois are slight, and often very inefficient implements; and, so far as I could learn, are constructed without much regard to any scientific principle. The farmers often manufacture their own ploughs, particularly the light one-horse ploughs, which are used for cleaning corn and ploughing land which has been reclaimed from a state of nature, when it is so light and friable that anything in the shape of a plough will stir it up. This light plough, when well made, is perhaps as well adapted for the country as any that could be introduced at present; as it is simple in its construction, and, when ploughing, it can be lifted and thrown about in any direction, to avoid the roots of scrubs, bushes, or any irregularity among the corn hills, which are very often far from being placed in straight lines. A stout boy could lift one of them on to his shoulder, and carry it with ease. When cleaning corn, this plough is drawn by one horse; but when preparing the land for crop, two oxen or two horses are used.

The prairie plough, though made much stronger than the small plough, is very seldom proportioned to the strain it has to bear; and, for the most part, makes wretched work. It is used only in breaking up prairie, and, when properly managed, takes a furrow of sixteen or eighteen inches in width, by three inches in depth, which is laid over quite flat with the grassy side down. By going so shallow, the plough is kept working among the very toughest of the rind; and the depth being graduated by two wheels which run, the one in the furrow, and the other on the uncut surface, if the several parts are not nicely and compactly adjusted, it must be obvious to any one at all acquainted with the principles on which a plough does its work, that the result must be very unsatisfactory. In fact, the work is often not more than half done; the plough being just as much out as in; and such an operation would be of very little use, were it not that the slightest displacement of the soil destroys the prairie grasses.* I have seen five yoke of oxen in one of these crazy creaking things, which, not unfrequently, are converted, by one smash, into a bundle of sticks.

Both of these ploughs are made much shorter than the Scotch plough. The beam in each is more upright, and the handles, in some instances, are nearly perpendicular. The share, sole, and breast are made of malleable iron, and generally all in one piece. The share (Scottice sock) is made as broad as the furrow intended to be cut, and is laid with steel beaten very thin, filed sharp on the outer edge, and tempered hard, in order to cut the tough roots of the grasses and weeds. The coulter, which is used only in the prairie plough, is also sharpened and tempered, and has on the under edge, near its point, a small socket, which fits on to a corresponding plug at the point of the share. The mould board is of wood. The wheels in the prairie plough act like those on the English wheel plough.

I am convinced that a good Scotch plough, with the share broader than that in common use, would break prairie much better than any of those I saw at work in Illinois; and this opinion is not confined to conjecture, as I saw at work one which had been taken out by a Scotchman. This plough, instead of being kept cutting among the toughest of the rind, was entered to a depth of six or seven inches, where the share was completely below the roots of the grass. By this means, the rind was divided by the sharpened coulter, whilst the share was working among the comparatively loose mould, without the slightest impediment, except when some grubs of hazel or other bushes came in the way. These grubs, when strong, ought to be taken up previous to ploughing; but in this instance they were mostly small, and were easily cut through by the share, which was sharpened on the right-hand edge, and was at its widest part as broad as the furrow taken.

The land ploughed in this manner in spring, was quite ready for planting wheat upon in autumn, and was, besides, effectually ploughed at once and for ever.

The native farmers had many objections to this plough; one was, that " it required to be held, and would not go alone as the prairie plough with the wheels did ;" another, that " it did not take a furrow nearly so broad as did their plough, and, consequently, did not go over so much ground in the day"—which is true, but then it does the work twice, and more than twice, as well. Ano-

* When the surface of the prairie is much trodden by cattle in wet weather the primitive grasses disappear, and the same result occurs when the grasses have been much eaten, or have been mown for a season or two.

ther objection was, that "no sod corn could be planted with it, as it would bury the seed so deep that it would never come up;" and this is true, if the seed were ploughed down, as is the practice with the prairie plough; but I believe that if the seed were sown broad cast and lightly harrowed in, it would procure a better crop than when planted by the prairie plough; and as a preparation for wheat in the fall, there is no comparison between the two methods. Yet, with all this, seeing that prairie is only to break once, it is very questionable whether it would be worth while to be at the expense of purchasing and conveying a plough from this country to Illinois.

Where labour is so valuable, people naturally attach much importance to despatch, and any method which serves to abridge labour, is seized upon with avidity. Of course, expediency is too much the order of the day, and people sometimes grasp the shadow and lose the substance. However, it ought always to be kept in mind, that in a country where labour is so dear, land so cheap, and nature so liberal, it is better to do a great deal in a middling way than to do a little well. The outlay consequent on tilling land with great care is not met by a corresponding return.

The horses in this part of the States are mostly small, bare-legged, durable animals, and more adapted for the saddle than for the heavier kinds of agricultural labour. As the prairies are quite free from stones, horses seldom require the protection of shoes; on the contrary, it is necessary at times to pare and reduce the hoof, which would otherwise grow too long, and be apt to break. I never saw a horse with unsound or diseased feet. As horses are much wanted, they are mostly broken at two and a half years old, which is, no doubt, the reason of their being so generally tractable. At corn huskings, and other gatherings, they are tied by the bridles to the branches of the surrounding trees, and will stand for hours. They are exceedingly hardy, and stand in stables pervious to every blast, and not one whit better than the woods, only they have roofs, which keep out the rain, and some of the snow.

The breeding of horses is a profitable business, as there is a ready market for them, and the expense of rearing them is trifling. When young, or going at large, they subsist very well on the prairie during two-thirds of the year, without any additional keep. They ought to have some artificial food during the rest of the time, particularly in the severe part of winter, which lasts from two to five or six weeks. Want of capital has hitherto been the cause of so little being done in breeding; but farmers,

as they begin to make a little money (unless the land-buying
mania seize them), generally keep a brood mare or two; and a
market is found at St. Louis or New Orleans for those exceeding the demand of the district. Such as go down to New Orleans
are floated down the Mississippi in flat boats.   The breed is
improving rapidly.

Cattle are a very mixed breed, being the produce apparently
of many European breeds combined, although in some places
they are evidently derived from the French breeds.   So long as
the country is unenclosed, no individual can, with any prospect
of success, attempt to improve his breed of cattle.   The prairie
is open to all, so that a number of herds come in contact in one
range; and bulls of all shapes, colours, and dimensions are going
at large, in spite of a county law to the contrary.   It may be
owing to the almost natural state in which they exist, that the
cows do not calve more irregularly, and at more inconvenient
seasons than they do; still, calves are frequently dropped during the severe weather in winter, when they are frozen to death
if not noticed in time, and carried to some place of shelter. The
tips of the ears are sometimes frozen off.   The calves are kept
up in some fenced place, as an inducement for the cows to come
home, which they do, for some time, pretty regularly in the heat
of the day and at night, when they stay till next morning at
sunrise.   When the calves are fed, one is let out at a time,
which instantly runs to its mother, and commences sucking at
one side, whilst the milker is busily employed at the other.   The
cows are frequently so very wild, that neither of the operators
derive much benefit.   As the maternal affection abates, the cows
become less regular in their visits, and finally must be *hunted up*
by a person on horseback.   It may readily be supposed that,
under such treatment, the calves do not make great progress;
and that in the fall and through winter, they are small, starved
creatures.

Some farmers, during severe weather, give their cattle a feed
of corn stalks or husks once a day; but many allow them to
shift for themselves. All kinds of stock would be much improved
by receiving fodder during the four months which, on an
average of seasons, constitute winter.   Under the present system of management, stock frequently suffers as much from the
want of water as from any other cause during severe weather,
when all the creeks and branches are frozen up; and very few
of the inhabitants put themselves to the trouble of cutting holes
in the ice, or of drawing water from the wells.

Cattle are subject to the *hollow horn*, a disease caused by

N

the severe frosts which injure the flint in the horn, and cause it to suppurate; when inflammation and death ensue, unless the horn is pierced so as to allow the matter to escape. Inflammation of the kidneys or red-water is frequently met with; and in some parts, there is a most formidable disease called *milk evil*, or *milk sickness*, which is not only fatal to the cows, but also to people who use the milk of the infected animals. The cause of this disease is not very obvious, but is generally supposed to be some vegetable of a poisonous quality. It may be as well to remark, that the evidence on this subject is of a nature so conflicting as to render the disease somewhat apocryphal; still I have heard it spoken of as a thing beyond all doubt by people who professed to have witnessed its effects. It is said to be confined to certain districts, where it appears only at irregular intervals.

As the system of rearing cattle is very bad, they are mostly small; yet I am inclined to think that, with proper management, a very good breed, and one quite as well adapted to the country as any that could be introduced, might be reared from them. They are very hardy, and far from being unkindly feeders; and I have seen many which might have been fed to 50 or 60 stones of 14lbs. It may readily be imagined, from what has been said of their treatment during winter, that they will not be in very good condition in spring, and yet many of them get to be very fair beef by the middle of June, and some by the end of May.

The steers, at three years old, when they become liable to an ad valorem tax, are sold off mostly to drovers, who take them to the state of Ohio to be fattened; whence they are finally conveyed to Philadelphia, and to other eastern markets. Droves of heifers are sometimes taken to the northern parts of the state; and towards Ouisconsin, where they find a market among the new settlers.

There is no difficulty in getting quit of cattle to almost any amount at these annual sales, and droves may be seen of 1000 or 2000 head. To be sure the prices are not large, but then the rearing costs almost nothing. This season (1841), the average price of steers and heifers was 18 dollars, or £3. 16s. 6d. sterling, taking the dollar at four shillings and threepence, and at this rate a yearly cast of ten head would bring in the sum of 180 dollars, or £38. 5s., a considerable sum in a country where living is so cheap, and the value of money so high.

The drovers come into the country in the beginning of summer, or as soon as there is a sufficiency of grass to afford a supply to the droves on their passage through the prairies and woods. After the drover has purchased as many cattle as he may want in a neighbourhood, a rendezvous is appointed, whither they are all to be brought on a certain day.

Few scenes in the west are more exciting than the start of a drove of cattle. On the evening previous to the appointed day, herds are seen approaching in all directions across the prairie, attended by men on horseback. Each of these herds consists of the entire flock of some farmer, who finds it a much easier matter to bring the whole than to select and force away from their companions such as have been sold. On arriving at the appointed place, where, of course, are the drover and his assistants, the cattle which are to remain are selected and driven into a strongly fenced enclosure, whilst their companions are allowed to return to their accustomed range, which they do without any force or guidance, striking through the woods or prairies directly for home, and at a speed which clearly indicates the small liking they have for such unwonted proceedings. A regular watch is set over the cattle through the night, in order to prevent them from breaking out; a feat which they sometimes accomplish in spite of all exertions to the contrary, when each makes the best of his way to his old range, and must be *hunted up* again next day.

I witnessed the start of a drove of cattle. At sunrise, all were in arms, and some droves might still be seen coming in from places near at hand. The sun was pouring his rays, almost blood red, through among the huge trunks and limbs of a neighbouring grove, tinging everything, and embuing the heaven with one rosy hue. Long diverging streaks of red might be seen escaping through some of the openings of the grove, and crossing, in mid air, over a green unwooded bottom, whose surface was yet wrapped in the stillness of early morning; whilst the ferruginous thrush, from the topmost point of a lofty oak, sung his matins in a rich song which echoed far through the silent woods. Horses stood hitched up to the branches of some young hiccory trees, which stood at intervals around the house, and men in the picturesque dresses of the West, and with heavy whips in their hands, stood laughing and talking in groups, or listlessly reclined against the rails of the fence.

The drover makes it one of the conditions of his bargain, that each individual from whom he buys cattle shall attend, or furnish some one to assist in getting the drove started, and fairly away, and in this instance there might be from twenty to thirty people.

At length all was ready, and the men mounted their long-tailed horses, and took up their positions in such a way as to interpose themselves between the cattle and the woods, and so force them out on to the prairie, on whose skirts the farm was situated. The barriers were pulled down, and out rushed the cattle pellmell amidst a torrent of shouts and yells. The charge was desperate, and for some time it was hard to say whether the beasts or their opponents would gain the victory; at length, however, with the assistance of their horses, many of which are beautifully trained to this occupation, it was evident that the men would succeed. Still the efforts of individuals of the herd were unceasing, and stray ones might be seen galloping on the prairie in all directions, horsemen dashing after them, shouting and belabouring them with their whips. One or two succeeded in getting into the woods, which were in some places filled with a thick growth of underwood, into which the horses fearlessly dashed, seemingly entering into the spirit of the chase. At length they were got fairly out to the prairie, and comparatively under command, although not by any means entirely subdued, as the drove was at full gallop and extended over a surface of half a mile. For the space of an hour they might be seen still making efforts to return, or to break off at one side, the horsemen galloping about, and plying the whip, whilst a distant shout rung faintly through the woods, and then they disappeared over a distant swell.

For a few nights, at the commencement of the journey, the cattle are shut up in some fenced place, and carefully watched; but ere long there is no need for such a precaution, as they appear to become resigned to their fate, and march on quietly through the pathless woods and prairies, browsing as they go; and if not overdriven, arriving at the end of their journey in better condition than when they started.

As there are few sheep, and very little care is taken of them, it is scarcely possible to judge how they might answer; but from what I saw of them, I am inclined to think they will become a profitable stock. Those reared at present seem to fatten readily, and to arrive at considerable weights, some from fifty to seventy pounds, and carry a good fleece of wool. The breed is almost nondescript, but very generally exhibits more or less of that distinctive mark of the merino, the tufted crown, although individuals occur of much larger bone than any merinos I ever saw. They lamb at all seasons, are never weaned, and are allowed to die of old age. Mutton is never seen at table, except at the house of some person from the old country or from the eastern states, and the natives cock their noses at it as we should do at a boiled rat. Sheep are kept solely for their wool. It is absolutely necessary in such a warm climate that sheep should be regularly supplied with water, and I firmly believe, that as many of them die from the want of that necessary as from any disease. In the dry season water is sometimes not to be found, except in pools in the creeks and branches. Horses, cattle, and hogs, can shift, if left at liberty, and will range for miles in search of water; but sheep neither can nor will take so much exertion, and seldom venture from the shade, from early in the forenoon till near sundown. I have seen them come and drink with the utmost eagerness when water was poured into the horse-trough at the well; and if ever large flocks are kept, there will be little difficulty in supplying them with water from wells which can be had, almost anywhere, by sinking no great depth; and a man will, in five minutes, pump as much as would serve some hundreds of sheep. It is necessary to house sheep at night, to protect them from the wolves.

The wool is mostly spun and manufactured by the females, and spinning wheels and a loom are very general items in a farmer's establishment. The principal manufacture is a sort of light cloth called *janes*, of which the warp is formed of cotton. Some of the women are very expert weavers, and employ their spare time in making cloth, which they sell or exchange for necessaries at the stores.

Fowls, of all the ordinary varieties, are reared in great abundance, and with very little trouble, and no sooner has spring fairly set in than the *old woman* has, chirruping in all directions, swarms of young ones, which in a short time form a very desirable addition to the universal meat, salt or smoked bacon. Eggs are collected, I may say, by bushels, and are much used. The eggs, fowls, and butter, not required for home use, are mostly either sold to men who go regularly about the country collecting such things, or to the storekeepers in the neighbourhood.— Sometimes they are sent to St. Louis, where there is a large daily market; the farmer making the journey, generally taking the produce of two or three of his neighbours, who accommodate him in turn.

On the subject of education, I again quote the work published by Augustus Mitchell:—

"The Congress of the United States, in the act for admitting the state of Illinois into the Union, granted to it the section numbered sixteen in every township, or one thirty-sixth part of all the public lands within the state, for the use of schools. The

o

avails of this section are understood to constitute a fund for the benefit of the families living within the surveyed township, and not the portion of a common fund to be applied by the state for the general purposes of education.   Three per cent. of the net proceeds of all the public lands, lying within this state, which shall be sold after the first of January, 1819, is to be paid over by the general government, and constitute a common fund for education, under the directions of the state authority.   One-sixth of the three-per-cent. fund is to be exclusively bestowed upon a college or university.   Two entire townships, or 46,080 acres, selected from choice portions of the public lands, have likewise been given to education.   Part of this land has been sold by state authority, and the avails funded at six per cent. interest.
*   *   *   The funds and claims of Illinois for education purposes may be estimated at 3,000,000 dollars.

"Provision now exists by law for the people to organize themselves into school districts, and to conduct the affairs of the school in a corporate capacity by trustees, and they can derive aid from public funds under the control of the state.   Upon petition from the inhabitants of a township, the section numbered sixteen can be sold, and the proceeds funded, the interest of which may be applied annually to the teachers of such schools within the township as conform to the requisites of the law.   To some extent the people have availed themselves of these provisions, and receive the interest of the fund.

"A material defect in all the laws that have been framed in this state, on this subject, has been in not requiring the necessary qualifications on the part of teachers, and a previous examination before a board of committee.   Without such a provision, no school law will be of much real service.   The people have suffered much already, and common school education has been greatly retarded by the imposition of unqualified and worthless persons under the name of school teachers; and were funds ever so liberally bestowed, they would prove of little real service, without the requisites of sobriety, morality, and sufficient ability to teach well on the part of those who get the pay.   *   *   *

"The people in any settlement can organize themselves into a school district, employ a teacher, and obtain their proportion of the income from the school funds, provided the teacher keeps a schedule of the number of scholars who attend, the number of days each one is present, and the number of days each scholar is absent, a copy of which must be certified by the trustees of the district, and returned to the school commissioners of the county semi-annually.   If the school is made up from parts of two or more townships, a separate schedule of the scholars from each township must be made out. The term 'township' in the school laws merely expresses the surveys of thirty-six sections, and not a civil organization."

I may add, that where the school sections are still undisposed of, or only partially so, the funds for education are very limited, and teachers, of course, difficult to be got; and in thinly peopled districts it is almost impossible to collect such a number of scholars as shall make it worth while, in a pecuniary point of view, for a person to commence teaching. When the number of scholars is likely to be too small to raise a remunerating salary, the inhabitants sometimes guarantee either to send a sufficient number, or to make good the deficiency in money. In the recently-peopled districts, there is often no school-house, and the teacher stays a week at a time at the house of each of his employers, such place constituting the school for the time being. The want of the means of education is one of the most serious drawbacks on immigration to the West.

An account of the government of the state of Illinois, and of the survey, sale, &c., of public lands, is given in the guide book already referred to, from which are derived the following extracts :—

" GOVERNMENT.—The constitution of Illinois was formed by a convention held at Kaskaskia in August, 1818. It provides for the distribution of the powers of government into three distinct departments—the legislative, executive, and judiciary. The legislative authority is vested in a general assembly, consisting of a senate and house of representatives. Elections are held biennially, as are the ordinary sessions of the legislature. Senators are elected for four years. The executive power is vested in the governor, who is elected every fourth year by the electors for representatives, but the same person is ineligible for the next succeeding four years. The lieutenant-governor is also chosen every four years. The judicial power is vested in a supreme court, and such inferior courts as the general assembly from time to time shall establish. The supreme court consists of a chief justice and three associate judges. The governor and judges of the supreme court constitute a council of revision, to which all bills that have passed the assembly must be submitted. If objected to by the council of revision, the same may become a law by the vote of the majority of all the members elected to both houses.

" The right of suffrage is universal. All white male inhabitants, twenty-one years of age, who have resided within the state six months next preceding the elections, enjoy the right of electors. Votes are given *viva voce.* The introduction of slavery is prohibited. The constitution can be altered only by a convention.

" The whole ordinary annual expenditures of the state are about 53,700 dollars. The revenue of the state is derived principally from land taxes. The tax of lands of residents goes into the county treasuries, for county purposes; while the tax on the land of non-residents goes into the state treasury, for state purposes. The quantity of land subject to taxation on the first of August, 1836, was 5,335,041 acres. And the quantity subject to taxation

In 1837 will be ...	...	5,674,452
1838 ...	...	5,902,127
1839 ...	...	6,262,367
1840 ...	...	6,616,380
1841 ...	...	7,837,218
And in 1842 about ...	...	12,000,000

" Lands sold by the general government are not subject to taxation under five years after purchase.

" PUBLIC LANDS.—The greater portion of the unoccupied lands of the United States constitute the national domain, and is, of course, under the control of the general government.   *   *

" The lands are surveyed on an accurate plan, and according to a general system; afterwards they are offered for sale by proclamation of the President, and, by law, must be sold by public auction, the minimum price being one dollar twenty-five cents. an acre, ready money. One section in each township is reserved for the support of schools in the township, and all salt springs and lead mines are reserved from sale, unless by special order of the President.   *   *   *

" The surveys of the public lands of the United States are founded upon a series of true meridians, which run north principally from the mouth of some noted river. These are intersected at right angles with lines running from east to west, called base lines.   *   *   * Each of these meridians has its own base line, which forms the base of a series of surveys, of which lines are made to correspond, so that the whole country is at last divided into squares of one mile each, and townships of six miles each, and these subdivisions are distributed with mathematical accuracy into parallel ranges.

" The greatest division of land marked out by the survey is called a township, and contains 23,040 acres, being six miles square. The township is subdivided into thirty-six equal portions or square miles, by lines crossing each other at right angles. These portions are called sections, each containing 640 acres, which are subdivided into four parts, called quarter sections, each of which, of course, contains 160 acres. The quarter sections are finally divided into two parts, called half-quarter sections, of eighty acres each; these, again, are under certain conditions sold in equal subdivisions of forty acres each, which is the smallest amount of the public lands disposed of by the general government.* Any person, whether a native-born citizen or a foreigner, may thus purchase forty acres of the richest soil, and receive an indisputable title, for fifty dollars. — The sectional and quarter-sectional divisions are designated by appropriate marks in the field, which are of a character to be easily distinguished from each other. If near, timber trees are marked and numbered with the section, township, and range, near each sectional corner. If in a large prairie, a mound is raised to designate the corner, and a billet of charred wood buried, if no rock is near.

" Sections are divided into halves by a line drawn north and south, and into quarters by a transverse line. The half-quarter and quarter-quarter sections are not marked in the field, but are designated on the plot of the survey by the Surveyor-General marking the distance on one of the ascertained lines in order to get the quantity of such half-quarter sections, as exhibited by his plot of survey.

" A series of contiguous townships, laid off from east to west, is called a range. These are numbered east and west from the principal meridian running due north and south. Townships are counted either north or south from their respective base lines.

" Sections, or miles square, are numbered, beginning in the north-east corner of the township, progressively west to the range line, and then progressively east to the range line, alternately, terminating at the south-east corner of the township, from one to thirty-six, as in the annexed diagram.

" The following will serve as a specimen of the nomenclature by which lots of land may be indicated in the system of the public land surveys. The north-east division in the larger diagram would be designated as section one, say of township four, in range three, east from the third principal meridian, and would contain 640 acres. The smaller diagrams, numbered 1, 2, 3, and 4, represent sections divided into portions of 320, 160, 80, and 40 acres each, respectively. The darkened division in No.

* I believe the general government grants only one purchase of forty acres to an individual.

1 would be designated as the east half of section one, of township four, in range three, east from the third principal meridian,

6	5	4	3	2	1
7	8	9	10	11	12
18	17	16*	15	14	13
19	20	21	22	23	24
30	29	28	27	26	25
31	32	33	34	35	36

and would contain 320 acres; the darkened division in No. 2 would be the north-east quarter of section one, township and range as before, and would be a tract of 160 acres. The darkened division in No. 3 would be styled the east half of the north-east quarter of section one, township and range as before, and would contain 80 acres ; the darkened division in No. 4 would be the north-east quarter of the north-east quarter of section one, township and range as before, and would be a tract of 40 acres. This is the smallest portion of the public lands sold by the general government."

All that a person has to do, when he has pitched upon a piece of land, is to find out its No., &c., as above, and apply at the land office of the district in which his lot is situated, when, by *entering it,* as it is termed, and paying ready money, he will become proprietor, and will in a few months receive from Washington city a patent or charter, signed by the President of the United States.

Improved lands, with houses, fences, &c., may be had almost at any time ; the price, of course, depending very much upon circumstances.

Only a small proportion of the public lands is bought at the sales by auction ; but after land has been offered at auction, it can be had by private bargain at any time, the price in such cases being invariably the upset one of 1 dollar 25 cents. per acre.

Specie is generally demanded at the land offices ; bank paper, however, if good, is received, though it is very seldom at par,

* Appropriated for schools in the township,

and the buyer has often to submit to a discount of from five to ten per cent.

Government lands are not taxable for five years after they are bought, and then are valued as first and second rate, the tax on the first rate being 3 dollars 20 cents. per quarter section of 160 acres, and on the second rate 2 dollars 40 cents. per do., or two, and one and a half cents. per acre, respectively. This tax goes into the state treasury; that on cattle and horses is appropriated by the county in which it is raised.

Taxes must be paid annually, on or before the first of August, the sheriff of the county generally fixing days at several of the most convenient towns in the district for that purpose. Though government is very lenient, yet if taxes are not paid up during two years, the land, or so much of it as will pay the taxes, with interest and costs, is sold, commonly for a mere trifle, as the first proprietor may redeem it at any time within two years of the time of sale, by paying double the amount of taxes, with the interest and costs. If the land have belonged to minor heirs, it is redeemable by paying the accumulated taxes at any time within one year beyond the time when the youngest comes of age. A " Tax Title" to lands, therefore, is not of much value; some, however, on account of the extreme cheapness of the purchase, are induced to buy, and, in some instances, no doubt get good bargains; but it is evident that such titles are liable to litigation, and that it is possible the claim may be disputed at any time within twenty years of the purchase.*

Horses and cattle are not liable to a tax till they are three years old; and the tax is an ad valorem one. There is no tax on sheep or hogs. Clocks and watches are taxed. There is a short yearly term of work, on the state roads passing through the county, required of each male inhabitant, a day or two for the most part being all that is necessary. In some counties I have understood there is a tax levied for the roads.

All the males between eighteen and forty-five are liable to serve as militia. When called out, the term of service is six months, with the same allowances as the regular army.

In their intercourse with one another, the inhabitants are much more courteous than the peasantry of Scotland or England, and maintain an ease and self-possession which is seldom seen, amongst what may be reckoned their equals, in this country. In

* In the instance where land is redeemable within two years, double the amount of taxes is paid, in order that the person holding by the tax title may receive some remuneration. I am unable to say whether such a course is followed in the case of minor heirs. I was led to understand, however, that where a claim of the latter kind was made good, the interim holder received no remuneration for improvements.

the West, distinction of classes is little known and seldom
recognised.　I have seen a veritable major invited to a corn-
shocking; and the major went.

There are not many amusements, at least what would here be
termed such; but among a people so simple and with so few
wants, little serves to please, and I have seen a number of
grown-up men playing at marbles with as much noisy zest as
would so many schoolboys in this country.　Saturday is often
set apart for some amusement, such as a shooting match, a
squirrel hunt, or a ride to some neighbouring town, where they
lounge about the stores and groceries, talk news and politics, and
sometimes drink a little.　There is an act against playing nine-
pins, which is evaded by making the number of pins ten, and
there are alleys in many of the towns.

Horse racing is a favourite amusement, and though not by
any means scientifically managed, is engaged in with quite as
much enthusiasm, and certainly with far less disastrous consequences, than that at Newmarket.　The distance run is mostly a
few hundred yards; perhaps a quarter of a mile.

The fourth of July, " Independence day," is a grand affair all
over the Union, when the pulsations of liberty arouse the nation
to its remotest extremities, causing some of these to cut very
curious antics.　I witnessed one of these exhibitions at a small
town in Illinois.　On arriving at the place, I found a considerable number of people in the stores, inns, and under any shade
that could be got from the rays of a most intense sun.　The only
stir in the dusty track called a street was about a well, which had
been so often disturbed by the descending bucket, that the water
had become the colour of gruel.　Conversation proceeded lan-
guidly, and as if all felt the mere act of breathing to be labour
sufficient for the time.　The purple martin alone seemed to enjoy himself as he swept past with his loud whistle, or fluttered
and chattered among a number of his companions, at the gable
of a frame house.

I stepped into one of the stores, which was full of men lying
about on the counters, or sitting on chairs, balanced on their
hind legs, the legs of the sitter being thrown upon the counter,
or something that brought them nearly on a level with his head;
a position which has been ridiculed by people in this country,
but which is not a little conducive to a fellow's comfort in a
warm climate, as it cools his parboiled feet by promoting a freer
circulation of the blood.

On a previous day, I had heard discussed in the same store,
the merits of the person (an unfortunate wandering preacher,

upon whom the towns folk had pounced,) who was to deliver the oration. The proprietor of the store addressed a man by asking if he had "heer'd Mr D—— preach last Sabbath?" "No," was the reply, "but I reckon he is a real first rater." "A mighty smart man, I tell you. The way in which he handles things is a caution. There is no dodging and going round about with him; he takes the straight shoot." "I wonder!" "We have got him to fix the oration for us, and he will do it well you may depend." "I expect." "I s'pose you will be here on that occasion?" "I reckon."

About noon, a considerable number of men and boys had collected in the street opposite the "house of entertainment," from which there shortly issued two fiddles and a flute, doing their best at "Hail! Columbia," and followed by the ladies marching in pairs. After the ladies had all passed, the gentlemen followed, in similar style. All was done with the most profound gravity; there was no hurraing, no laughing nor talking, nor indeed any sounds save those proceeding from two very bad fiddles and a flute, and the crowd of martins overhead. It would have been considered the very height of indecorum had one of the beaus offered his arm to any of the ladies. I am far from objecting to gravity of demeanour on an occasion like this. The commemoration of the freedom and independence of a people ought to elicit feelings which are not to be exhibited in noise and tumult; but the demeanour I have alluded to prevails at all public meetings of the sexes, and is a national trait.

The procession left the town, and entered the forest, where, after having proceeded about a quarter of a mile, it halted among some trees, whose foliage tempered the rays of the sun to a mellow light. It was a truly fine temple of liberty. In an open space, among the tall stems, stood a waggon, into which mounted the orator, and another gentleman who introduced him to the audience. The oration consisted of what one might have supposed to be a series of unconnected scraps, the reminiscences of previous and similar occasions, and was delivered in a hesitating, unanimated style, which contrasted strangely with the bombast conveyed by the words. Indeed, the man seemed, to use one of their own expressions, "to be in pretty much of a fix." The audience sat or lay at full length on the ground, the ladies on one side of the waggon, and the gentlemen on the other, whilst some boys, or rather little men, for the boyhood of America seems to be as short as its spring, were overlooking the whole from some bushy trees.

There was no drunkenness or riot consequent on this occa-

Q

sion; indeed, the first example of drunkenness I saw in this
neighbourhood was in a grocery to which I was attracted by the
sound of a fiddle, where, on entering, I found the barkeeper
playing " old coon" to a tipsy man who was dancing; and this
man was an Englishman. Any other examples I saw, and they
were few, were of reputedly worthless characters.

Very many of the young people are taught sacred music;
and " singings" are frequently held, during the fall and winter,
at the different farmers' houses; and when a fiddle can be had,
there is a dance, otherwise some game, such as hunt the slipper
or forfeits, concludes the amusements of the evening. I never
saw any drinking, nor the slightest approach to riot, on these
occasions.

A store, in this part of the country, and indeed in America
generally, is a grand melange of things of the most different
qualities, as it proposes to supply the inhabitants with all the
necessaries and luxuries they may require. They are sources of
great profit; and a person with a little capital and some know-
ledge of the business, can scarcely fail, with ordinary prudence,
to realize an independence. The prices charged for goods of
the most ordinary quality, are truly exorbitant. There is a
difference of from ten to fifteen per cent. between ready money
and credit.

A grocery is not by any means what the name would imply
with us, for, although it may be the receptacle of tea, coffee,
and sugar, it is not invariably so. It is, in fact, a dram shop;
and very often is entirely devoted to the selling of spirits.

Grist mills are much wanted, and form a capital investment
for money. The average charge for grinding is now about one-
sixth, which, with wheat at 75 cents. or a dollar per bushel, is
great pay. The motive power is chiefly steam or oxen. The
ox mills are driven by a large wheel inclined from the horizontal at about an angle of 20°. Around the segment is a broad
gangway, on which the oxen are placed, and tied by the heads
to a cross bar, which is independent of the wheel. The weight
of the oxen thus acting on the inclined gangway, puts the wheel
in motion, whilst the animals, in order to retain their position,
a e obliged to step forward. In order to stop the wheel, a drag
with a lever is applied to its circumference.

Good saw mills are profitable concerns, 1 dollar 75 cents.
ready money being charged per 100 feet for oak plank of one
inch, and two dollars on credit for a few months; whilst three
dollars are charged for walnut and some others of the scarcer
woods, such as curly maple, &c. Timber is sometimes sawed

on shares, when the logs are hauled up to the mill, and one-half of the quantity is given in payment for sawing. A good steam saw mill may be erected for from two to three thousand dollars; and a good steam grist mill, with two pairs of stones, elevators, cooler, &c., complete, for from six to eight thousand dollars.

I think wind mills might be erected on the prairies with great chance of success, as the wind blows very steadily; and at almost all seasons, even in the hottest weather, there is a breeze during most part of the day. The only objection to such mills would be the thunder-gusts, which come sweeping up with a thunder-storm. These are truly formidable, and sometimes clear an entire gap out of the forest, level fences, unroof houses, &c. The thunder clouds ordinarily follow up or down the rivers and large watercourses, when they travel slowly; but sometimes a portion of the cloud is seen to separate from the rest, and to strike across the country in a line at an angle to the course of the river; and these, as far as my experience goes, are invariably swept along with a thunder-gust.

Thunder-storms are much more frequent, and more severe, than in Britain. At some seasons it thunders for several days and nights, and during these times the sound, near or remote, never ceases. I have counted six different clouds in view at once, and have heard it asserted that a person may sometimes walk a quarter of a mile in the darkest night, and never lose sight of the ground. I certainly have been out during the night when the interruptions were at such wide intervals, and of so short a duration, as not to cause any impediment to the traveller. The light is of a greenish blue. The lightning very often strikes almost perpendicularly, but I think most frequently in a direction nearly horizontal, when, if it come in contact with a dense cloud, it is smashed into a number of small streams, which fly off at an angle to its previous course.* The lightning strikes very frequently in the woods, and it appeared to me that at least two-thirds of the dead trees had been killed by the electric fluid. Some of the trees had merely some limbs and bark torn off, whilst others were shivered down to the earth, the remaining part of the stump being jammed till the fibres were separated as if they had been pounded with a mallet. During my stay, a young man was killed, and a barn and houses set fire to in the neighbourhood.

The climate of Illinois is warm in summer, which, in the southern parts of the state, lasts about six months—from the begin-

* When the lightning took this appearance, a Scotchman with whom I was frequently in company, used to exclaim, " Aigh, there's the tawse !"

ning of April to the end of September. The mean temperature of summer for a series of three years is said to have been, for the southern half of the state, 74° 34′ of Fahrenheit. However this may be, there is very little doubt that the thermometer, in the generality of seasons is, during July and August, frequently from 90° to 98°, and sometimes 100° in the shade.

During summer there is almost always a refreshing day breeze on the larger prairies, whilst the woods are hot almost to suffocation.

From September to the first or second week of December constitutes the fall or autumn; whilst what remains may be called winter, although it is seldom that there are above two or three weeks, and sometimes only a few days of severe weather. As the change from winter to summer is very sudden, there is little spring.

The fall is by far the pleasantest season of the year, as the nights become cool and refreshing, and the days are mild with a cloudless sun, except during what is called the "Indian Summer," when the atmosphere becomes dull and smoky, and the sun is shorn of his rays This peculiarity in the American autumn sometimes lasts nearly a month in the West, and is, no doubt, caused by the burning of the prairies. I am aware that this theory has been objected to, and that it has been urged, that the effect of burning the prairies could never extend to the eastern states; but when we consider the immense extent of these prairies, and how very generally they are overrun by fire, I think we may fairly doubt the accuracy of such a conclusion. It is well known that in 1783, an eruption from the mountain of Skaptaa Jokul, in Iceland, gave a smoky appearance to the atmosphere, and tinged the sun, which in colour looked like blood, in Great Britain and over a considerable portion of the continent of Europe. With this fact before us, I think it not unreasonable to conclude, that the burning of a dense crop of herbage, over an extent of thousands of square miles, may produce results somewhat similar.

On the breaking up of winter commences, what may be termed, the rainy season, the most disagreeable period of the year, when, for a short time, the country is almost impassable, from the fulness of the creeks and branches, and the deepness of the roads. The temperature of this season is exceedingly variable, the thermometer frequently ranging from 30° to 70° within the twenty-four hours. Early in March, during the time I was in the country, the thermometer one day stood at 85°, and in 35 hours was down at 32°, with heavy snow.

The prevailing winds in summer are from some of the points between south and west; those in winter range from north to north-west. Easterly, north-easterly, and south-easterly winds are not frequent, and seldom continue for many hours together. I never experienced anything like a continued gale; although during winter and spring, there was sometimes a stiffish breeze which lasted a day or two. The north-west wind is the coldest and by far the steadiest. It seems always to be on the alert, and to be restrained for the time only by force, as, if any extensive atmospheric changes take place, it frequently, even in the warm months, succeeds in giving a puff or two. The thunder gusts are of short duration.

The diseases which seem peculiar to the climate are mostly those of a bilious character and ague. In sickly seasons, bilious fever prevails. When properly treated, ague, though often a lingering disease, and one causing much debility, is not fatal; but bilious fever sometimes assumes an aggravated character, when it speedily carries off a number of victims. Worms (lumbrici), are exceedingly annoying to children, and frequently to grown-up people, and it may be doubted whether they are not a more frequent cause of derangement and disease than is generally supposed. However this may be, they rarely fail to occur in children who have been debilitated by disease. Much disease is evidently the result of a want of precaution; a proof of which exists in the very general opinion, in places which have been inhabited for some time, that fever and ague are on the decrease. Now it can scarcely be supposed that any change can have been made in the climate in so short a time, by a few inhabitants, whose operations are a mere scratch compared with the extent of surface over which they are scattered, particularly when it is considered that in the prairies timber increases rather than diminishes with the progress of settlement; but it is evident that the comforts of the settler have become much increased; that many good brick, frame, or log houses have taken the places of the miserable shanties and huts of the first settlers; in short, that there is, comparatively, ease and abundance in place of unremitting toil and exposure, added, perhaps, to meagre diet.

In the summer months there is a disease of frequent occurrence, called "prickly heat;" a sort of nettle rash common to hot climates.

Exposure to the heavy dews is a frequent cause of ague.

With a little prudence, and a few medicines, with which every settler in the West ought to be provided, along with a know-

R

ledge of the proper dozes to be prescribed, an immigrant of sound constitution may avoid much sickness, and enjoy almost, if not quite, as much good health in Illinois as in this country.

Whilst good physicians are rarely to be met with, there are many desperate and unprincipled quacks, whose universal nostrum is calomel, which, Sangrado-like, they administer on all occasions, and in large dozes. No doubt a hot climate requires the exhibition of calomel in larger dozes than could with safety be used in more temperate latitudes ; but there are to be met with in Illinois, frequent instances of people whose constitutions have been ruined by the incautious use of that drug.

When travelling on horseback through a thinly-peopled part of the country, I fell in with one of the inhabitants, who, as he told me, "had taken *the crïtter* (horse), and Sunday as it was, had been to the mill, as his family were almost starved out for want of meal. There had been such mighty hot times, that the ox mills were all at a dead fix from the oxen having given out." On putting the common question, if there was much sickness in these parts, he replied, "Well, a tolerable deal." "Is it fatal ?" "Pretty considerable I reckon ; me and the doctor has had hard times of late." "Indeed." "Yes ; and although I aint none of the riglar doctors, I know the way how to kill ague better than many a doctor by a long shoot. The old doctor— he's a mighty smart man—often trusts his patients to me to finish them off, when he has more than he can manage." "Finish them off— how ?" "Why, he jest stops the fever, and I prevent a dilapse, and we set them on their feet in the shelling of a corn-cob." "You cure them all ?" "Well, pretty considerable, till of late, when the doctor got a new assistant, who ought to be dogged to death : he killed two men right off. The doctor sent him to see them, and he never did nothing till one of them began to get skeary, and sent for the old doctor ; but it was out of time ; the man's inside was gone, and the other was the same way. The assistant put out that same night. We did hear since, that the man was no doctor after all, but jest a tailor's man who had run away from his employer and turned doctor ; and I reckon he made a bad start." "But why did the old doctor not examine him, and make him produce satisfactory testimonials ?" "Well, he had some such thing as a letter, but it was a forgery, and as for examining, the old doctor was so everlastin' busy, he hadn't no time."

I do not think it probable that the average duration of life is so long in Illinois as in more temperate climates. The human race comes sooner to maturity, and evidently begins to decline at an earlier stage than with us, and, to an old countryman, the natives very generally appear several years older than they really are. A man of eighty is not often to be met with.

When a death occurs, the funeral takes place in not many hours after, a circumstance rendered necessary by the heat of the climate. Any of the neighbours may attend the funeral if they think proper, but none are invited, though it is expected that those in the immediate vicinity will come. Unless the death is very sudden, the news of it are speedily conveyed through the neighbourhood by the women, who evince great alacrity in attending and sympathizing with the sick, it matters not whether strangers or friends. Alas, how much genuine feeling and hospitality is rubbed off in the process of civilization! To be sure, a London or a Birmingham is rather too much for one heart.

There are few public burial grounds, and, for the most part, a family selects some spot on the farm, as a place of sepulture. I was one day wandering through the woods in search of deer, when, in a lonely spot, overshadowed by some large oaks, I stumbled on five graves. There was no inclosure, nor anything to indicate the presence of a burial ground, beyond the unequivocal shape of the mounds, and a few split rails arranged over each, to prevent the attack of the numerous bands of hogs which roam at large, or of wild animals. A feeling of awe came over me, such as I never experienced even in the solemn aisles and time-honoured fanes of England, with all their associations.— There was a sense of complete seclusion—a silence befitting the last repose. There was nothing pertaining to existence to distract the attention; the face of the earth, beyond the mere graves, was still under the dominion of nature; there was no busy hum of voices—no " clack of a distant mill ;" there was not even the sound of an axe, whose stroke is heard far through the silent woods, whilst the light shed through the thick foliage of the lofty trees was in perfect keeping with the whole. I afterwards learned that this was the burying place of a family who lived on the borders of the prairie.

CHAPTER V.

The buffalo, or bison, has disappeared from Illinois, and the nearest points at which he is now to be found are on the head-waters of the Mississippi, and on the extensive prairies between the Missouri and the Rocky Mountains. This animal flies from the approach of the white man, and, to his delicate perception of smell, the atmosphere becomes tainted by the first approaches of civilization. His home is the wilderness; but whither shall he flee from the rapacity of man? It has been estimated that " at present from 150,000 to 200,000 of these noble animals are slaughtered annually for the sake of their skins," and that " in ten years they will be all killed off." The doom of the buffalo, and of his native master, the red man, is sealed. So late as the commencement of this century, there was plenty of buffalo in Illinois, and the paths which they made in their annual migrations, and the *licks*, are still quite visible. The paths are narrow, and in a direct line from the inland prairies to the large rivers. A lick is, frequently, an extensive depression with an abrupt termination at one of its sides, towards which the other sides shelve gradually inwards. The place is not necessarily a puddle, nor, in many instances, does it contain any saline admixture perceptible to the sense of taste. The attraction seems to be a fine greasy clay, of which a stratum is always to be found at the dry licks, and which is like fuller's earth. The tame cattle at present on the prairies frequent the licks, where they may be seen, not only licking, but scooping out the clay with their teeth. What are termed *salt licks*, are formed by salt springs, which are numerous in some parts of the state.

The elk has disappeared from the state, but plenty of deer remain in most parts of it, and are said to increase in number, up to a certain point, with the population of a district, and this is accounted for from the protection afforded them from wolves, which are eagerly hunted and soon become thinner, as there is a bounty of four dollars a scalp given by the government.

The American deer, somewhat like the hare with us, is not easily driven from his range, and a buck may be noticed, a long time, frequenting the same localities; he sheds his hair twice a year, and is in summer of a pale red, and in winter of a dunnish brown, or, as the hunters term it, *blue.*

The bear and cougar, or panther, as the latter is commonly called, are not plentiful in the prairie districts, and are soon killed out. They frequent districts covered with dense and extensive forests. The meat of the bear is highly prized by the hunter.

The wolf, most common in the prairies, is the grey or prairie wolf, which is destructive to sheep, hogs (when young), and calves. Packs of them are frequently heard through the night, howling and yelping, and their near approach is easily ascertained by the dogs about the house, which bark and howl alternately with rage and terror. It takes a dog to be very fierce, and regularly trained, to face a wolf on any terms, and I have known one which would have engaged with anything else, turn tail and run home from his master, on crossing the fresh trail of a wolf on the prairie. Few dogs, singly, are a match for a wolf, which, if he can get a chance, will run down and devour a dog as he would do any other prey.

Wolves seldom attack man, and then only when they are pressed by hunger, and are in large packs. The smell of blood is a great inducement for them, and if a man be carrying game, or be wounded, or incapacitated from shewing a bold front, they will sometimes attack him. A person with whom I was acquainted was returning one evening in winter from the woods, where he had been chopping, when he heard a pack of wolves in full cry, and soon became aware, from the course they were pursuing, that they were upon his trail. He was lucky enough to have got up into a tree just as they arrived, and so disappointed them of their prey, though they howled round the tree, and detained him there during the whole of a severe night, and only departed at sunrise, when he got home almost starved to death. Such occurrences, however, are so rare that people never think of calculating upon them.

The wolf, though a ferocious and sanguinary animal, is a coward in the main; for, if once fairly entrapped, he will not shew fight, but will, unresistingly, permit himself to be stabbed, or beaten to death with a stick.

Beaver, once in great plenty, are now nearly extinct in the state.

The racoon abounds, and is very destructive to Indian corn, which it attacks as soon as milk is in the ear.

S

A *coon hunt* affords capital sport for the boys, who, when night has fairly set in, sally forth with the dogs, which are generally well trained to the business. On arriving at a corn field, whilst the hunters stand on the outskirts, the curs are silently directed to range, when, if they find, they instantly start full cry after the game, which makes for the woods, and ere long takes to a tree; a circumstance of which the hunters become aware from the peculiar bark of the dogs. As the darkest nights are selected for the sport, tumbles and other mischances are frequent in the rush made towards the spot indicated. When the tree is reached, materials are collected for making a fire. The flames soon gather strength and dispel the darkness, which seems only to have retreated, and to have added to the deepness of the shadows. And now many an anxious face and peering eye is directed towards the limbs of the tree in search of cooney, who, at length, is discovered perhaps huddled into some crotch. If the hunt is possessed of a rifle, poor cooney soon has his *flint fixt*; but if the axe is the only weapon, his fate is not quite so soon decided, for the tree may be large, and when cut down, he sometimes will escape through the mellee, and succeed in gaining another. Four or five are sometimes killed in a night.

The opossum is frequently met with, and as it is a sluggish creature, is easily captured. On receiving a thump, he cunningly shams death, which circumstance, and his reported inroads on the henroost, subject him to an exterminating persecution.— People who attempt to deceive are said to *play 'possum*.

The skunk is frequently seen on the prairies and in the woods. He leaves his hole about dusk, and wanders about in search of prey through the night. Woe to any one that comes too near him, for, though not a savage animal, yet he possesses a means of defence which procures him a very general exemption from annoyance, and of which the effects long remain as a memento of his prowess. Unlike the generality of heroes, the skunk enters into battle *stern on*, as they say at sea, and by the discharge of a most noisome fluid, soon brings the affair to a matter of flight or of suffocation. If any one is so unfortunate as to have his clothes sprinkled with this fluid,

" The wide sea
Hath drops too few to wash *them* clean again."

Indeed, the natives assert that nothing, save burying in the earth for some time, will destroy the stench; and it is very doubtful if that, or anything short of burning, will accomplish its destruction.

Most dogs require only one lesson to make them ever afterwards very cautious how they approach an enemy who uses such unhandsome weapons, and whose discomfiture is productive of nothing but disgrace, as they are, for some time after all such engagements, kicked and beaten from house and home. Some *real varmints*, however, can never be restrained. Dogs are said to have been killed by receiving the discharge in their mouth; and I have known one roll over and foam at the mouth, as if in convulsions.

The skunk is somewhat larger than a cat, not very active, and of a brownish black colour. Most of them have a white stripe on each side, extending from the head backwards; in some specimens the white is the prevailing colour. It is said to feed upon fruit, and the young of birds and small animals, and sometimes visits the henroost; indeed, it is by no means shy, and will occasionally get into the cellar below the floor of the house, when all possible respect is paid to it, and a summary process of ejectment is never resorted to.

A friend of mine, returning from hunting deer one evening, happened to fall in with a skunk, and being anxious to have a closer inspection of the animal than he had previously obtained, decided upon shooting it dead upon the spot, and so preventing it from making a discharge. He was only partially successful; for though the shot proved fatal, the usual consequences of interference took place. Determined not to be baffled, he approached, nose and stick in hand, and turned the creature over once or twice. Being aware that the shooting a skunk would be a standing joke among his hunting acquaintances, he determined on keeping the affair a profound secret. On his approaching home, several people happened to be lounging about the door, in the cool of the evening, who, when he came close up to them, with one consent exclaimed, "Ah! you've been killing a skunk! you've been killing a skunk!" For a while he put on an enquiring and much-injured look, requesting, with some hesitation, to know what they meant; but the truth was only too palpable, and he made a merit of necessity by joining in the laugh against him. The unpleasant sensations arising from most smells can be avoided by stopping the nose; but the smell of the skunk affects the throat with a feeling of tightness and suffocation, even when inhaled by the mouth. After all, the stench is exceedingly disagreeable, but I think not quite so intolerable as is sometimes represented.

The mink or polecat, which is very like our foumart, is plentiful, and very destructive to poultry. When it gets in among the young broods, which are unable to fly up to the trees, where the fowls roost in summer, it exhibits its sanguinary nature by destroying as many as it can get at.   On one occasion I happened to be a witness to its devastations at a farmer's house on the prairie.   Like the other loghouses of the country, this was raised some distance from the ground by blocks of wood placed beneath the corners, consequently there was some space between the floor and the earth.   The surrounding space, between the bottom logs and the ground, was built up, except at one corner, where a hole was left to admit the young broods, which resorted to the place at night.   It was night, and I had been in bed some time, when I heard some chirrups and half-stifled squeaks beneath the floor.   There are so many chirruping frogs and crickets, with other insects, making noises through the night, that I had no suspicion of what was going on, until one of the old fowls began to flutter and beat with its wings most furiously.   I instantly leapt over the bed, and, by stamping on the floor and shouting, endeavoured to frighten the creature from its prey.   The farmer and his wife, who heard the fray, and suspected what was the matter, instantly joined me from the other end.   The hole at the corner of the house was stopt up, a light procured, and the puncheons torn up from the floor.   The thief was now fast, but not a whit daunted; for in the midst of the most active operations of his assailants, and whilst running from one part to another to avoid the pokes and blows aimed at him, he never missed an opportunity of throttling a fowl, if it came in his way.   Owing to our inability to raise all the floor, he had a good deal of cover, and the battle raged a considerable time.   At length it was proposed to shoot him; and one of our party leapt down into the cellar (a hole dug down through the earth beneath the floor), and brought his face and head to a level with the space between the floor and the surface of the ground.   Here, with candles placed beside him, he watched an opportunity, and at length shot the mink.   Our forces, including both sexes, amounted to five; and as there had been no time to think of dressing, the scene, when the excitement was over, looked rather queer.

On reviewing the field of battle next morning, it was found that there were eighteen killed, and one young *rooster* "rendered," as Mansy Waugh said of the goose, " a lamiter for life."

The American hare, or rabbit, as it is commonly called, is exceedingly numerous where the country has been settled for some time, and is very destructive to young fruit trees and other garden produce.   It is about the size of the English rabbit, of nearly the same colour, and when caught cries like the hare.— It does not burrow, though it is frequently found in the hole of the ground hog or American badger, and in hollow trees, to which it runs for shelter when raised from its form and pursued. Half a dozen of them may be taken in an hour, with the assistance of a dog, and an axe to cut them out of the trees. They are very fat in the fall, and are quite as good for the table as our rabbit.

Of squirrels there are, in the West, the fox, grey, flying, and ground squirrel or chip-munk. The fox squirrel is considerably the largest, and is of a red colour, the fur along the back being tipped with white, like the fur on the back of a fox. The grey squirrel, though not so large as the preceding, is considerably larger than that common to Great Britain, and is a very sprightly and beautiful animal. The flying squirrel is small, and is covered with a very fine fur, ash coloured on the back, and of a dirty white below. With the exception of a few points of contact, it has the power of inflating, like a bladder, the skin over all its body. The skin is extended from each side as far as the wrist of the fore and hind legs; and this part being stretched out with the legs, and also inflated, there is afforded a considerably diminished specific gravity. In this state the animal leaps from the upper limbs of a tree, and floats gracefully through the air, for a distance of perhaps fifty or sixty yards, before coming to the ground, or to the lower part of the trunk of some other tree, when it allows the air to escape, and the skin falls close to the body, except between the fore and hind legs, where it hangs somewhat loosely. The flying squirrel is a gentle creature, possessing only a very small portion of the activity of its kind. The ground squirrel, as its name implies, does not climb trees.

The fox and grey squirrels are highly prized as an article of food, and are shot through the head, to preserve the body from being spoiled by the bullet. The meat, particularly of the grey squirrel, is white and tender, and the bones are of delicate pink colour. They are sad thieves in the corn fields and corn cribs.

The wild turkey is found in great numbers in many parts of the state, and is a noble bird. The colour of the male is dark, in some parts of the body, approaching to black, with very beautiful coppery, golden, violet, and purple reflections. The colour of the female is somewhat lighter than that of the male, and not so brilliant. This fowl has not been improved in size by domestication, but, on the contrary, seems to have degenerated. Fifteen pounds may be stated as the average weight of the male, though Wilson says " birds of thirty pounds are not very rare," and that he has " ascertained the existence of some

T

weighing forty." They are the shyest of game, and, to hunt them with success, requires experience and dexterity. In the spring mornings, the hunter secretes himself behind some log in the bottoms, which the birds frequent at that season, and with a call made of the bone of a turkey wing, or a bit of elder with the pith out, imitates the cry of the hen. If any of the *gobblers*, as the males are called, be within hearing, they instantly gobble, and, if they have no suspicion, run towards the sound, and on its being repeated come close up, sometimes mounting the log behind which the performer is concealed. Great care is necessary lest the slightest movement, click of a lock, or rustle among the leaves be made, as on any such occurrence the bird makes off at a speed which defies pursuit. The hunter frequently searches for them at night, and finds where they roost by crying like the barred owl, when they reply by a gobble. The young broods are flushed by a dog, when they take to the trees, and with proper caution a shot may be had.

The turkey is not very apt to take wing in his flight from an enemy, and at some seasons will not do so; but nature has endowed him with a power of limb which is a sufficient security against any dog of ordinary speed. I have known an instance of one being chased about three miles, and then lost, although it was pursued by a man on horseback, attended by two very stout and active dogs, quite accustomed to the business. The chase commenced in the open prairie; the man having got between the bird and the woods.

The pinnated grouse (prairie chicken) may be seen in flocks of hundreds on some of the prairies. It is of about the size and of nearly the colour of the female of our black cock, and might easily be mistaken for it by a person not well acquainted with the British bird. The male has a tuft of feathers on each side of the neck, which he can erect and depress at pleasure. Beneath these are two bags of yellow skin, which the bird can distend with wind till they are about the size of small oranges. At the commencement of the breeding season, and during the morning and evening, the males frequent particular spots, where they strut about with erect tail, ever and anon stretching out their necks, distending the orange bags, and uttering a peculiar sound, called by the people *bum-booing*. By this sound it is quite impossible accurately to judge of the distance at which the fowl may be. I have heard them at all distances, from fifty yards to half a mile, and, paradoxical as it may appear, without the use of my eyes, should have found it very difficult, if not impossible, to judge of the relative positions of the performers.

How far the sound may be heard I cannot say; but in a calm morning it can easily be heard a mile.

This fowl is excellent eating, and is caught in traps in great numbers during severe weather, and the hunter will sometimes condescend to shoot a few with his rifle, although he thinks it a waste of powder and lead.

The quail or partridge is very abundant among the older settlements, and seems to accompany man, and to increase as the country becomes improved. Though much less than the English partridge, it is quite as good, and is a plump and very pretty fowl.

Quails are caught by scores, in nets of a conical shape, and of considerable length. When being used, the net is distended on hoops, and placed on the ground, in a favourable situation among the the bushes. To hunt quails it requires two or more men on horseback, who, having seen their game and set their net, ride cautiously around, hemming in the birds on all sides except that on which the net is placed, and very often succeed in driving them into it. The bird is very tame, and is more inclined to run than to take wing from the presence of man, particularly if he is on horseback. They are in coveys of from ten to twenty or thirty.

At the seasons of migration, the whole air is filled with multitudes of swans, cranes, geese, and brants, and ducks of various kinds. Great havoc is made amongst them at the lakes and ponds by those possessing smooth-bores.

The passenger pigeon, of whose surprising multitudes most people must have read, has roosting and breeding places in some parts of the state.

The barred owl is held in evil odour, on account of his visits to the henroost. It is a large, powerful bird, measuring from three to four feet in extent, and can easily fly off with a good large chicken. Fowls, except in severe weather, roost on the trees in the neighbourhood of the house, and if an owl once commence his depredations, he will repeat his visits nightly, until, in some instances, not a fowl is left. The only way of getting rid of the offender is to watch him some moonlight night, and to shoot him. It would appear that only a few of this species turn robbers of henroosts, for if all that are seen were blameable, it would be quite impossible to preserve fowls, without shutting them up every night.

Fishing with the seine is sometimes practised in the ponds and lagunes in the bottoms, such places being connected with the rivers, and receiving a new supply of fish at the freshets; but, although caught in great numbers, the fish are by no means good. The seine is used only when the rivers are so low that the ponds are unconnected with the main stream.

Shooting fish with the rifle is a pastime sometimes resorted to, the sportsman getting upon some elevated bank, or in default of that, on a tree overhanging the lake, and watching till the fish rise to the surface of the muddy water to bask in the sun, when he fires at them, and, as some of them are large, frequently succeeds in hitting them. A fish is sometimes killed without being touched by the bullet, the concussion of the water, it would seem, being in such cases sufficient.

Among the novel discomforts of the West, that of insects is one of no trifling character. The whole earth and air seems teeming with them, and mosquitos, gallinippers, bugs, ticks, sand-flies, sweat-flies, house-flies, ants, cockroaches, &c., join in one continued attack against one's ease. No sooner do those who wage war during the day retire, than their place is filled with others, labouring with equal effect through the night, whilst the indefatigable mosquito, in many situations, heads the attack at all times. Half worried through the day, you are glad, when night comes, to get rid of your clothes and the crawling things you have felt on your skin. You get rid of the ants, which, however, do not bite, but seem to be exploring, and they explore the very bottles by eating down through the corks; but the ticks require a more summary process, and, if they have been allowed to remain many hours, can only be got rid of piecemeal. These ticks sometimes cause a troublesome sore, and being in myriads in the long grass, there is nothing for it but a regular tick hunt every night. As some novels relate of their much-afflicted heroes, you " go to bed, but not to sleep," for, after having in vain tried to oust the mosquitos, first by puffing and blowing, then by striking right and left, then by exposing nothing but the tip of your nose at the risk of being smothered—the thermometer at 90°—you begin to summon a little patience, and are willing to compound for some sleep, by the loss of a little blood.— This heroic resolve is scarcely formed when a combined attack of bugs from all quarters, apparently attracted to a centre of which you are the focus, settles the question, and unless you are an Indian or a Dutchman, drives you to the floor with a blanket. After a few hours of fevered rest, day and the sun's rays almost simultaneously burst through the crevices of the loghouse, and sleep is banished by a continued cackling and crowing of fowls, and stirring about of the inmates of the house. Having poured a basin of water over your neck and head, you feel somewhat refreshed, and think it possible that you may be able to take some breakfast. The old woman gives the signal, and in you go from the bars or fence surrounding the house, where you have been lounging, and trying to enjoy, in spite of a *few* mosquitos, the comparative coolness and beauty of early sunrise. The house is no sooner entered than you hear one continued hum, and the room is almost darkened by myriads of house-flies, which, in Illinois, are never seen out of doors, and which, when there are sick people in bed, require the constant attention of some assistant to drive them off, otherwise, if the patient were a child, or very weak, I believe they would soon suffocate him. Molasses, sugar, preserved fruit, bread, everything on the table, is loaded with them, and the very operation of fanning them off drives numbers of them into the molasses and other things of an adhesive nature. It is not safe to open your mouth. It is evident too, on examining the molasses, that the small red ant has been purloining it, and has left a number of his unfortunate companions enveloped in its mass ; whilst ever and anon a cockroach makes a dash at the table, and, in nine cases out of ten, succeeds in scampering across over meat dishes and everything that comes in the way, and that too in spite of the bitter blows aimed at him with knife and spoon, he is " so t'rnation spry."

Snakes are numerous, but, with a few exceptions, are quite harmless. For one rattlesnake, or other snake of a dangerous character, twenty harmless ones may be seen. Every one does his best to kill a poisonous snake, and in not many years after a district begins to be peopled such reptiles become rare. Rattlesnakes are very plentiful on some of the rocky bluffs, where they get shelter through the winter, and are then sometimes found in holes, coiled up by scores together, in a torpid state. The inhabitants recognise two kinds of rattlesnake, to wit, the wood and the prairie rattlesnake, or mississauga, of which the latter is much the smaller and less dangerous. Indeed, I believe the danger resulting from the bite of these reptiles is, *cæteris paribus,* very much in the proportion of their relative sizes ; the large ones bite deepest and infuse most poison into the system. The bite of a rattlesnake is sometimes fatal, though by no means invariably so, and with proper remedies may be got over at the expense of some fever and inflammation of the adjacent parts. The Indians have several *snake-weeds,* some of which they use, by poulticing, to allay the inflammation (it may be by neutralizing the poison), and of others make decoctions, to be drank by the patient. The hunter's cure is not a bad one ; as soon as possible after being bitten, he pours from his horn some gunpowder, which he ignites upon the wound; should the first application fail to raise a blister, he repeats the operation till a blister is raised. By puncturing the blister, and applying poultices of snake-weed, much of the poison is extracted from the wound.

When the rattlesnake is irritated, he coils himself up and shakes his rattles, which are situated at the extremity of the tail, and which produce a sound somewhat like that of a grasshopper. When attempting to bite, he can only uncoil himself to his full length. The word bite scarcely conveys a proper idea of the process by which a snake inflicts a wound, as there is no closing of the jaws at the time, but merely a stroke, very similar to that given by the foot of a cat, by which the two fangs in the upper jaw of the reptile are driven into the victim, and sometimes scratch the skin for some distance. The poison is communicated to the wound by a groove along the lower side of the fang, which is situated above the poison bag in the jaw.— When the snake strikes anything, the tooth presses against the bag, and the poison is injected through the groove. The fangs lie flat till the mouth is opened to a certain extent, when they begin to rise, and are nearly at right angles to the jaw when the mouth is at its full width, at which time the lower jaw is so far thrown back as to be in the same line with the upper one. The fangs are somewhat hooked, as sharp as a needle, and, in a snake of three feet, may be about half an inch long.

The rattlesnake is very thick and heavy in proportion to its length; and, although it is sometimes seen from six to eight feet, is mostly met with from two to three feet long. There are several other poisonous snakes; among others, the yellow moccasin and copperhead, of which the latter is not plentiful, but is said to be more poisonous than the rattlesnake. None of these reptiles attack man, but act merely on the defensive, and, for the most part, try to get out of the way.

It is said that hogs kill and eat snakes, and there is a very general belief that these animals suffer no injury from being bitten. How far hogs may be constituted to withstand the effects of a snake's bite, I know not; but I have seen snakes offered to them, and never saw them pay the slightest attention to the reptiles. On one occasion I carried a snake alive from the woods to a herd of swine lying near the bars of a farm house; on throwing it down among them, the hogs took no notice of it, but another and most unexpected antagonist entered the lists— no less than one of the old woman's roosters. The snake was lying at length on the ground when the fowl noticed it, and each to have an instinctive and mortal antipathy at the other. No sooner did the cock see the snake, than he put himself in an offensive attitude, the snake at the same instant rearing himself up and darting out his forked tongue. After a number of feints and inefficient blows on both sides, the cock at length succeeded in giving his opponent a severe blow with his beak on the back part of the head, which laid him prostrate in an instant. After two or three more heavy blows on the same spot, to make all safe, the victor picked the snake up, and ran off trailing it, and pursued by a number of hens pecking and pulling at it. From their manner, it appeared to me that the hens wanted to eat the snake; and, had it been small enough, I have no doubt they would have done so. Deer are known to kill snakes by bounding on the top of them with their feet.

CHAPTER VI.

In a work like this, it may be thought unnecessary to say much about hunting; more particularly as it ought not, in the slightest degree, to influence the intending emigrant. The hunter is always poor, and in some measure despised by his more industrious neighbours; and when a man once acquires a habit of wandering in the pathless wilderness in search of game, it takes such hold of him that he very rarely shakes it off; indeed, the occupation requires a vigilance so absorbing, as speedily to characterize his whole manner. The old hunter's eye is never at rest; meet him where you will, in the forest or within the walls of a house, and whilst he is conversing with you, his eye will be wandering, slowly and intently, from object to object; and if on his feet, he will be constantly shifting his position, and, with his head and shoulders depressed with habitual caution, will repeatedly sweep the entire circle of vision.

The real hunter is the pioneer of American civilization. He is the first to dispute the possession of the wilderness with the red man and with the wild denizens of the forest, and in some measure, like them, is intolerant of the near approach of a population, bringing with it the trammels and interruptions of civilized institutions. The sound of the axe in the woods is hateful to him; and no sooner does the smoke of the settler's fire become frequent in his neighbourhood, than, packing up his scanty moveables, and placing them in a vehicle of most primitive construction, he with his family seeks a more congenial home in those solitudes where nature still holds undisputed sway. He buys no land, nor asks any one's leave to build his hut or till his little corn-patch.

> "The free-born forest, found, and kept them free
> And fresh, as is a torrent, or a tree."—*Don Juan.*

Let not the inhabitant of the crowded city think, that in doing this the hunter makes any great sacrifice; he is merely giving way to the impulse of habit, and choosing what is most agreeable to his tastes. He was born in solitude. No busy hum of men—no " sound of church-going bell" ever saluted his young ears. All his feelings, all his reasonings, are influenced by the loneness in which they were conceived. His associations are not tinctured with the busy crowds and homes of cities, but with the still solitudes of the primeval forest. He has not learned to philosophize on the ebbs and flows in the destinies of congregated millions; but he has wandered and mused on the banks of some leviathan river, rolling its waters along, whither he knows not, whence he cannot tell,—a dream, a mystery.

Your true hunter is often a simple-minded, unaffected child of nature; true, he is ignorant, but this ignorance includes the follies and very many of the vices of civilized life. The worst example of his tribe is he who has not fled before the influx of population, and who, impatient of the restraints of industrious habits, has generally reaped nothing from civilization beyond its vices and its scorn.

The hunter of the West generally follows his occupation on horseback; and a more picturesque turn-out, or one more in keeping with the accompanying scenery, is not often to be met with. He generally wears a broad-brimmed palmetto hat, covering a profusion of hair, which flows over his neck and shoulders. His face, tanned by exposure to all weathers, is often garnished by a beard, untouched by razor or scissors for many weeks, and his throat, unless the weather is severe, is unfettered by a neckcloth. His capot, made from a Mackinaw blanket, generally blue or pale green, has the broad grey border fantastically arranged about the cuffs, neck, and between the shoulders, whilst his capacious trousers, of home-made janes, have their nether extremities stuffed into the tops of his long-legged boots, made somewhere *down east*. Slung over his shoulder is a bullet pouch made of leather, or of the furred skin of some wild animal, ornamented with sundry tags and fringes, accompanied by a powder flask, made of a fine horn, and polished so thin, that the grains of powder can be seen through it; a charge or powder measure, made of horn or bone, with an attempt at carving upon it, and often with the initials of the owner's name; and a tomahawk, with its head enclosed in a leather case. In the front part of the belt which sustains the last-mentioned articles, is a sheath containing a large knife. The other shoulder is occupied by a heavy rifle, with a barrel of fifty inches long, stocked forward to the muzzle, and mounted with brass. The but, in some instances ornamented and inlaid with silver, is hollowed out into a crescent shape at the extremity, so as to sit securely on the arm, and thus to act as a counterpoise to the leverage of the muzzle.— The horse, like its rider, is "unkempt, unshorn," with flowing mane and tail, caparisoned with a double-reined bridle with Spanish bit, heavy and plated with brass, and a Spanish saddle with heavy brass stirrups; a blanket being folded for a saddle cloth.*

Riding leisurely along the outskirts of the prairie-girt grove, he is seen to stop at a point commanding a view of some sweeping vista embayed in the dark woods, like an arm of the sea, with many winding channels of green among the bosky islands of hazel, sumac, and sassafrass. Long and patiently he stands searching the openings with his practised eye to catch a glimpse of the browsing deer. If, after waiting a considerable time, he sees no game, he moves to some other point; but if he should happen to see a deer, he slips from his horse, and, by taking advantage of any inequality of the ground, or of intervening bushes, and by keeping the game between him and the wind, tries to get within shooting distance, and is generally pretty secure of his object at one hundred and twenty or one hundred and thirty paces, if his rifle is not of very small calibre. Should the deer run off, the western hunter rarely attempts a running shot; but should he succeed in killing his deer, and not be desirous of procuring any more, he goes for his horse, which is broken to stand for hours where it is left, and, having pulled the deer up before him, takes it home. If the deer be too heavy for him, or he wish to continue his hunt, he cuts a forked sapling with his tomahawk, strips it of its top and branches, and having bound the hind legs together, slips them into the fork, and raises the carcase against a tree, to a height sufficient to secure it from dogs and beasts of prey; or, adopting another method, he climbs up a slender tree, and bending its top to the ground, secures the deer to it, not too near the top, by the hind legs, when he lets go, and the elasticity of the tree raises the slaughtered game to the height required. At his leisure, he returns with a small light sled or a cart, and conveys the fruits of his hunt to his dwelling. In cold weather the carcases of deer are sometimes allowed to remain in the woods for a week.

From what I have heard of the red deer of Scotland, he must be a much shyer animal than the American deer; indeed, if you can keep out of sight or smell of the latter, he is not at all

* This description applies to the best appointed of those hunters who have remained among the settlements. The hunter on the frontier settlements is often clothed in a hunting shirt, leggings, and moccassins of tanned deer skin.

times inclined to run off at the snap of a stick, or at the rus-
tling of leaves, although on hearing these sounds he will stand on
the alert, with his head thrown back over his shoulder, and his
nostrils distended, gazing steadily in the direction from which
they proceed.   But, should he catch the slightest sniff or glance
of a man, he throws his flag, or single, as the tail his called, in
the air, and with a sort of sharp snort, approaching to a
whistle, darts off, crashing through the bushes, and bounding
over their tops.

The Kentucky rifle I have in some measure described above,
yet I may add a few particulars, seeing the weapon has acquired
some celebrity.   Whatever the calibre may be, the barrel is
very rarely below forty-five inches, much more frequently forty-
eight or fifty, and sometimes longer than that, and often so
heavy, that to hold it out steadily, requires an arm of no little
strength.   Rifles for shooting deer and other large animals
carry about forty bullets to the pound; the bullet in such
instance being nearly half an inch in diameter.   More rifles,
however, are to be met with below than of this size, and they
are to be seen so small as one hundred and twenty.   Those
from eighty to one hundred and twenty are used for shooting
turkeys, squirrels, and other small game.   Though for the most
part accurately cut, they are coarse in material as well as work-
manship; and notwithstanding their great thickness, they not
unfrequently burst,—a circumstance which, to me, appeared quite
mysterious, until I detached one from the long stock, which
completely covers the lower side of the barrel, when the mystery
was solved.   It would appear that the barrels are made from a
bar of iron, the edges of which are brought together, and
welded,—a process which might answer well enough if the welding
were efficiently performed, which it never had been in any
instance that came under my notice; but, on the contrary, was
sometimes so badly done, that it was surprising that the gun
ever withstood the shock of a single discharge.   The breach,
like that of the musket, is without any breach-piece in the stock,
which is of curly maple.   The lock is a coarse thing, whose
retail price in this country might be three or four shillings, and,
among the old steady hunters, invariably flint, with a double
hair-trigger.   Such an article as I have described will cost forty
dollars, about £8. 10s. sterling : I am sure it could be made in
England for forty shillings.   Snapping is the order of the day, and
I have seen a fellow snap five times in succession with the most
imperturbable coolness; but that was nothing,—I met a man in
the woods one day, who shewed me his lock, nearly a new one

and which he told me had only fired *once*, and really that once may be ranked among the many mysterious ignitions of gunpowder which we read of; the lock, springs and all, being made entirely of iron.* A regular hunter never buys a flint, but searches for small thin pieces of that material about the creeks and branches, and these he prefers to any hammered ones.

There is no use in trying to argue a western hunter out of conceit of a long barrel; indeed, he looks with contempt on anything below forty-eight inches, or that has not a muzzle as thick as a horseshoe: he "do'sn't believe in a short barrel, it won't carry up." Doubtless, owing to the slowness of the gunpowder they use, a barrel of considerable length may be of some advantage; but to prolong to forty-eight inches, a barrel carrying one hundred and twenty, or even one hundred to the pound, is downright nonsense, and I never saw any of them, which, at eighty yards, would do much more than pierce through the bark of an oak, or make a crack louder than the whiffle of an air-gun. The effect of the charge is nearly thrown away in overcoming the friction of the bullet, and in expelling the column of air from the bore. I would, however, by no means confine the length of barrel to the point of maximum effect (i.e., where the expansive force of the charge has diminished till it has become equal to the friction and other retarding causes); but would sacrifice a little power, in order to secure greater accuracy of aim, which is much more attainable with a barrel of some length than with one which is very short. For, if the bore and the line between the sights be in the same plane, any error committed in taking the sights with the long gun, will not be so great at equal distances as will the same amount of error committed with the short one; in other words, the angle included between the line of error and the true line, will not be so great in the long as in the short gun. Another advantage obtained by a barrel of some length is, that, owing to the leverage of the muzzle, a steadiness is obtained which cannot be accomplished by adding weight without length. Very considerable strength is essential in a rifle barrel, more especially when long; for, otherwise, it is apt to warp when being discharged, and weight lessens the recoil, which ought never to be very sensibly felt. When shooting off-hand, a slight barrel will shoot with sufficient accuracy, but with a rest, and a hunter, when stalking, is sometimes so placed that he cannot help resting his piece, it is apt to make random work, if the material rested on be hard, as wood or stone.

Though the western hunters all agree in preferring long bar-

* This might be one of the "one shilling locks" mentioned by Mr. Babbage.

rels, there is much diversity of opinion regarding the calibre.—
It appeared to me, that each was very much in the habit of
preferring that calibre to which he was accustomed.   So far as
my own experience extends, and I have used rifles of various calibre, I prefer, what in this country are termed, small sizes;
and if I had my choice, would not use a rifle carrying below forty
to the pound; and, when the barrel is well made, and the scroll
accurately proportioned to the calibre, should prefer one much
smaller. A well-proportioned rifle, carrying eighty to the pound,
is a very efficient weapon for shooting anything from a deer
downwards, as it combines the qualifications of not tearing small
game, and of being sufficiently powerful for deer at a considerable distance.   I am aware that many people in this country
will be startled at this assertion, but I have had very considerable experience in the use of such a gun, and know that it will
send a bullet through a deer at one hundred and thirty yards,
and break some bones into the bargain.   Another advantage of
such a gun is, that for the same weight of lead, you have two
shots with an eighty, for one with a forty bore; a matter of
small moment about home, but which, when a hunter is outlying
for deer, and has everything to carry about with him, is not a
matter of indifference.

Some hunters prefer rifles termed *tearers*—a qualification
which, I believe, is given them by increasing the twist of the
scroll, and thereby causing the bullet to make a revolution on
its axis in shorter space than it would otherwise do.   Such guns
it is said, are more deadly from making a larger wound; but it
is evident that, owing to the increased friction in the barrel, they
cannot shoot so hard, unless the charge be increased, and that
endangers the stripping of the bullet.

I do not know the proper twist for the scroll, nor did I ever see
any treatise on rifles that threw much light on the subject.   One
evolution in forty-eight inches, or, when the barrel is shorter than
that, at an equivalent rate, I have heard accounted the best
twist; but it is evident that this, although it may be applied to
a number of different bores, will, with perfect accuracy, suit one
only, for there is a very great difference between the inclination of
a scroll performing one evolution, in a barrel of forty-eight inches,
with a bore of half an inch, and the inclination of a scroll, performing an evolution in a barrel of equal length, but with a bore
of an inch.   From this it appears that it is necessary to carry
the scroll oftener round, in the same distance, in a small bore,
than in a large one.   The plan for ensuring accuracy would be
to make experiments with a bore of any size; and, after having

found at what angle with the direction of the bore, the scroll most efficiently insured force with accuracy, to cut the scrolls of all rifles, of whatever calibre, at that angle.*

In this country, great stress is laid on the charging of rifles. The method the hunters take of finding out the proper charge of every new supply of gunpowder, is one of the best.—— If a stranger goes up to the door of almost any house in the backwoods, and looks about him, he rarely fails to see, at the distance of twenty rods, a tree hacked and hewed, sometimes nearly through; it is the shooting tree, and the hacking is done with the axe to get out the bullets. When the hunter gets a new supply of gunpowder, he tries his rifle with it at this tree, and graduates his charge so that it at least carries up, i. e., shoots point blank, at twenty rods,—a desideratum which, in a very long gun of large bore, is not attained without a heavy charge, which may, in part, account for the frequent instances of bursting formerly mentioned. A patch of six hundred linen, well greased on the side exposed to the friction of the barrel, is forced in with the bullet, which ought not to be so tight, that it cannot easily be entered and sent home with one hand. No mallet for entering the bullet is ever used by the hunters, and yet I never knew of their bullets stripping, nor do I think it possible to make rifles to shoot with greater accuracy. In taking aim, the feet are set wide apart, and the body thrown back upon the right leg, the right elbow is raised, till the arm is perpendicular to the body, and the hollowed end of the but inserted at a short distance from the shoulder, the left arm being extended to its full length along the stock. At the commencement of taking aim, the muzzle is considerably depressed; but, on the sights being arranged, is gradually raised, with a motion decreasing till it terminates, and the gun is discharged at the same instant.

The rifles constituting the scroll are very shallow in American barrels, and when they become too much worn to be serviceable, the hunters, by a very simple process, cut them out again. A hiccory rod, somewhat smaller than the bore, is introduced into the barrel, and placed in its centre. Around the rod melted lead is poured to a height of ten or twelve inches, which completely envelopes it, entering, at the same time, into the rifles. When cool, this plug is driven out, and retains in relief on its surface,

* Mr. Wilkinson, whose work on "The Engines of War" I have seen since writing the above, states the military standard for rifles in England to be two feet six inches for one revolution; but, seeing the calibre is not mentioned, this information gives no precise data for ascertaining the angle which the rifles constituting the scroll make with the direction of the bore.

the scroll, which acts as a guide in the operation of cutting. A steel cutter, about half an inch in length, and accurately fitted to the rifles, is inserted into one of the relieved parts on the plug, and padded behind with slips of paper, to which more are added as required. By means of the rod, the plug is worked from end to end of the barrel, each rifle being deepened in turn.

In the Eastern States rifles are met with of all lengths and sizes, but are almost invariably shorter than those in the West. The barrels are frequently of German manufacture, and some, which are highly spoken of, are made of cast steel. Some rifles there are carrying five or six charges, which can be fired in succession, but such of them as I saw were truly Yankee notions, and deserving of being classed with the wooden nutmegs.

CHAPTER VII.

Having sent our heavy luggage by New Orleans to New York, my friend and I started from St. Louis on the third of September, tolerably mounted, and our *plunder* reduced to a pair of saddle-bags a-piece,

St. Louis, in Missouri, is situated on the right bank of the Mississippi, and eighteen or twenty miles below the junction of that river with the Missouri. There is here a daily and extensive market for all country produce, which drains a large portion of the surrounding district, within a distance of sixty or seventy miles. Large quantities of pork, fowls, eggs, butter, game, fruit, &c., are disposed of for ready cash. The city, of course, requires a considerable supply, but the numerous and crowded steamers are doubtless the cause of such a constant and large demand. There is a regular influx of waggons, particularly towards evening, as the market, like most markets in the States, commences early in the morning.

The city* contains a very mixed population, whose character is " as well as can be expected." Murder and robbery in the city and its neighbourhood are by no means uncommon. It was here that the populace forced the prison and seized a negro who had stabbed a white man. It would seem that a regular trial, and the punishment of hanging, were thought too good for a slave who had dared to raise his hand against a white man, and Lynch law and roasting alive were substituted in their place.†

* The population of St. Louis in 1830 was 5,852, and in 1840, 24,585, shewing an increase of 18,733 in the ten years.
† An incident connected with this tragedy which I heard, but do not vouch for the truth of, struck me at the time as being remarkably characteristic of the dogged endurance frequently displayed by the negro.— It was related thus:—On being conveyed to the place of execution, namely, the forest adjoining the city, the poor wretch was bound to a tree, but at such a height above the fuel, that his lower extremities were all but consumed before his vital parts were much scathed. The ropes which bound him to the tree at length being burnt through, the poor creature fell with a crash down through the burning mass and disappeared.—

A murder was committed in the neighbourhood a short time before our arrival, and another victim, who had been stabbed in a bar-room on the previous night, died on the day of our entering the city. It would be unjust, from such instances of depravity, to infer that there was no respectable class of society in St. Louis, and my intention in stating them is merely to shew that there exists a class capable of commiting the blackest crimes, and which at times sets the law at defiance. Indeed, what may be termed the orderly class, is but too apt to execute Lynch law, an instance in corroboration of which occurred whilst we were in the neighbourhood, in the destruction, by the populace, of some houses of ill-fame, which had become a public nuisance.

Judge Lynch is a somewhat ticklish fellow to be entrusted with the fasces, and yet it says a good deal for him, that he more frequently uses the insignia of the tar-pot and bag of feathers, than of the bundle of rods and the axe, though, in his haste, he does sometimes dress the wrong man. Brother Jonathan goes so fast ahead, that the law has no chance to keep up with him, and so he does his own law, and soon becomes so expert that he can scarcely be hindered from legislating for, and enlightening others.

St. Louis stands on a pretty steep bank, and looks very beautiful from the opposite side of the river, which is a mile wide.—The waters of the Missouri and Mississippi are here quite distinct, the former being of a brown, and the latter of a pale yellow colour. Large steamers are very frequently arriving and departing, and there is a constant bustle of lading and dislading at the levee. The city is supplied with coals from the bluff on the Illinois side of the river, to whose bank they are conveyed a distance of six miles, by a railway across the American Bottom. A steam ferry-boat plies constantly through the day; the fare is about sixpence sterling.

Immediately opposite St. Louis, the American Bottom is twelve miles wide, in some places densely wooded and intersected with ponds and back-waters, and in others, consisting of prairie, interrupted by groves of pinoak (laurel oak), hiccory, persimmon, paw paw, &c. The plain, in many places, abounds with those ancient mounds which are so frequently met with in many parts of the States, and which here in some instances run in a continuous line for a considerable distance. They may range from ten to thirty or forty feet in height, and there is one which is said to be ninety feet; but which appeared to me to be consider-

Some one ran forward, and, looking into the flames, cried "he is done for now." "No," answered a calm voice from the centre of the flaming pile, "I am not done for yet."

ably higher. Their shapes are various, some being conical, others oval, and others more or less angular, whilst some have buttresses carried from the base to the top, giving the mound a fluted appearance. The large mound* above alluded to has a platform running round the south side, at about half its height, and the cone which rises from this is flat on the top. The base, whose circumference is said to be six hundred yards, appeared to be a polygon, but of how many sides I did not ascertain, as I could not ride round it for fences and corn fields. The earth, for the construction of this huge mass, has been lifted from the circumference of its base, as is evident from the regular ditch-like depression intervening between it and the surface of the prairie.—On the north side, which I could not get at, it appeared to me that the ground naturally fell away towards a creek in the immediate neighbourhood. It is not unlikely that the immense ditch contained water, which has either been drained away artificially or by the natural depression of the creek. Water sometimes occurs in the depressions of the surface, which, so far as I saw, invariably accompanied, and were always proportioned to the size of the mounds. The large mound is sprinkled with trees, and there is a level space on its top, where some one has built a nice-looking frame house, from which there must be an extensive view of prairie, bluff, and forest. From the great quantities of bones said to be contained in some of these mounds, it is very probable that the small ones of them at least had been used as places of sepulture, and, perhaps, those even of large extent, but of no great altitude, were used for the same purpose; but there can be little doubt, from the size and construction of others, that they were intended for places of defence. There are some large specimens in the city and neighbourhood of St. Louis.

The heat and dust in crossing the bottom were truly oppressive. As the tracks from different parts of the state towards St. Louis converge and coalesce, the passage upon them becomes very considerable, and the dust gets beaten to an impalpable powder, which the slightest movement raises in clouds. The traveller's clothes soon become so completely powdered that it is difficult to distinguish their original colour, and, as he perspires freely, his face acquires the hue of a chimney sweep. Our horses were tormented with *greenhead* flies, which suck their blood, and by the bots fly, which, though not a bloodsucker, is, to a horse, the most intolerable of insects. This fly, which is somewhat like

* I believe this is the mound called "Monk Hill," from the circumstance of some monks of the order of La Trappe having sometime resided upon it. They left it in 1813, and returned to France, whence they had fled during the Revolution.

our gad-fly, in its colour, size, and mode of flight, deposits its eggs on the long hairs of the back part of the fore leg, between the knee and the pastern, on the flanks, and generally, wherever the horse can reach with his mouth, so that, in scratching himself, the eggs may be introduced and swallowed with his food; from these eggs, bots (the fly in its larva state) are produced, which cause so much distress to horses, and which finally pass through and become the fly. The places of deposit, particularly those above mentioned, frequently appear quite gray, from the number of eggs. The fly is very wary and very dexterous in its operations. After flying about for some time, as if reconnoitering, it approaches some particular spot, and, poising itself in the air, in an instant has deposited an egg upon a hair, from a flexible oviduct, and is away fifteen or twenty feet. The egg seems to adhere by some glutinous matter. By what secret sympathy the horse becomes aware of the operation, I know not; but the moment the fly touches the hair, which it does on the wing, never sitting down nor adhering, he starts as if struck with a spur, snorts and rears, and sometimes becomes quite unmanageable. A horse which will endure, without flinching, the united attack of scores of greenheads, will become quite outrageous at a touch, so very slight, that I never could distinguish that it even bent the hair.

There are, on this part of the American Bottom, a good many enclosures, and some straggling villages, whose population, in one or two instances, is almost wholly French; the descendants of the original explorers of this part of the country. The ancient bluff is, in some parts, denuded of trees, and consists of a series of sharp-pointed knobs clothed with grass, and looking in the distance like a range of hills.

On approaching the bluff, which was here covered with forest, our horses mended their pace, as if anxious to gain the shade. We had hardly entered the woods, and begun to climb the steep ascent, when our ears were saluted with a loud halloo; and, on looking to the right, we saw sitting on the grass, in a deeply-shaded hollow, three people with a waggon and two horses.— "Strangers," cried a man of the party, holding up the remains of a water melon about the size of a half moon, "may be you'd like to ate a little uv this?" As the proposal was a most agreeable one at such a juncture, we acceded to it at once; and having hitched up our horses, joined the party, which turned out to be a man with his wife and son, who came from the neighbourhood of Vandalia, and were thus far on their return from market at St. Louis. In conversation, we learned that the man was originally from Ireland, and that he had settled at first in one of the Carolinas, from which he had lately removed to his present location near Vandalia. On asking him why he had removed from the South, we got the old story, that a man who had not a number of slaves and a large estate was *despised* by the planters, and was, in fact, almost deprived of society; as those who considered themselves above him, would hold no intercourse with him, and those of his own class were comparatively few in number.

In the afternoon we reached Collinsville, a town of a few years old; but which, like the young men in this country, had quite as much pretension as if it had existed for centuries. It contained a church, a sabbath school, a mill, a store, and the never-failing *hotel*. Mr. Collins, a down-easter, and the founder of this notion, kept the hotel, which was one of the cleanest and best it was our fortune to fall in with for some time; to be sure, when we asked where the stable was, we were told "he hadn't had time to get it fixt up yet, but there was a most a beautiful black-jack oak, through which the sun couldn't shine no how." Mr. Collins, thinking we were on the look-out, expatiated at great length on the many advantages, and the salubrity of this neighbourhood, and of Collinsville in particular; indeed, he made it appear that folks must have been most unaccountably blind, not to have sooner discovered its many most estimable qualities. In spite of his assertions, however, there was much sickness at this time, not only in less favoured parts, but, if we might believe our eyes, among the inmates of the Collinsville Hotel; but these, Mr. Collins said, were boarders, who had come from St. Louis to get cured.

Leaving Collinsville, we arrived after sundown at Troy, on Ridge Prairie. On being shewn to bed in the only hotel of the place, we found the end of the room where the gable should have been entirely destitute of that architectural feature, so that we had an uninterrupted view of the stars, and the benefit of any chance breeze that might be stirring, whilst the indefatigable catydid serenaded us through the livelong night. The bats, with whose nightly visitations, in search of house-flies and mosquitoes, we had long been familiar, and whose wings are frequently heard flapping within a few inches of the face, might here come and go without being put to the trouble of creeping in and out at some cranny.

Here we fell in with two Missouri drovers, who had been at Kentucky buying sheep, and were on their return with about three hundred of these animals of an impure merino breed.

There are, as yet, no large flocks in Missouri, and these men proposed getting quit of their drove by selling it in detail, in small numbers, to the newly-settled farmers in the neighbourhood of St. Charles, and on the Riviere au Cuivre, in Missouri.

Our horses had not yet been shod, and as we were about to enter on a thinly-peopled district, we thought it necessary, as a matter of precaution, to have that operation performed here where there chanced to be a blacksmith's shop. The Vulcan of this modern Troy was a little broad-faced Frenchman, who hammered and chatted away with equal facility. On my mentioning the sickness so prevalent at the time, he remarked, " it is all very true, de sickness has been great, but ve have de doctor; ah, he is a mighty smart man! I reckon de vay in vich he can cure de fever is a caution ven he is sober; but he is an old seaman, and likes de cogniac. De oder night he vas sent for, but he could not go, as he told dem he vas hard aground; however, dey insist, and lift him on his horse, and put out vid him von on each side. Ah, he is a mighty smart man."

During the time the horses were being shod, there rode up to the shop door a young man, who, for some time, sat moodily watching the operation. At length he said, " Well, Mr. Dupin, I reckon you heard about that ere frolic at Bates's the other evening ?"—the blacksmith nodded assent—" and that Tom Jervis and me had a fight, and Tom whipped me ?" Another nod from the smith, who seemed desirous of saying as little as possible. " But if it hadn't been that I was the worse of liquor, and he got me down, the way in which I would have walked into him would have been a caution. I'd have whipped him like forty; but I'm not done with him yet, and I'm on the hunt for him to-day, and if I can't whip him I can shoot him, and here's the thing that can do it." Here he pulled from the pocket of his capacious trowsers the brass-mounted but-end of a horse pistol, at which the little blacksmith gave a furtive glance, without pausing in his operations. " I'll shoot him as cold as a cla'-bor (clapboard), and 'taint far to Missouri." After some more conversation of a similar nature, and of which a large proportion consisted of the most dreadful backwoods imprecations, the fellow departed. The blacksmith stood, hammer in hand, looking after him some time, and then giving his shoulders a silent shrug, went on with his work.

The prairie in the neighbourhood of Troy, in Madison county, is perhaps as rich as any that we saw during our journey, and the corn and other crops were of excellent quality. Much of the corn was from twelve to fifteen feet high, and it was easy to see, from the stubbles, that wheat had been excellent. In answer to a question I put, a person told me, that a field had yielded at the rate of forty bushels per acre; this, however, I did not believe, for although it was evident that the crop had been a good one, the number of bushels stated was far beyond anything that came within my own experience. From all I saw or could learn, it would be unsafe to calculate on more than twenty-two bushels per acre. We found that it would not do to place implicit confidence in the information we got from strangers, for travellers making enquiries about the capabilities of a district, are always understood to be on the look-out for a location, and many of those already located are willing to sell, and it is obviously the interest of all that a neighbourhood should be soon peopled.

On leaving Troy, we fell in with a man, who told us that he had moved to this neighbourhood from the famous Sangamon county, and that he liked it better, as the land was equally good, and it was easier to fall in with a suitable farm than in Sanga-mon, which was nearly bought up and mostly peopled by Yankees, whom he did not like. This last objection I had pre-viously heard stated, and the western people generally seem, I think unfairly, prejudiced against their eastern countrymen, who are decidedly the most enterprising farmers in the West. They may be a little too " slick" for the Illinois *suckers*.

There is a tract of country here, comprehending parts of the counties of Madison, St. Clair, and Randolph, which I have frequently heard said, will bear comparison with most districts in the state, as regards capabilities of soil and situation.

A few miles to the north-east of Troy, we entered on the Marine Settlement. This settlement, which is situated on a large and beautiful prairie, consists of grants, which, we were told, had been made to retired officers of the American navy. The face of the country is high, undulating, and well watered, and the district is said to be healthy. The houses on this settlement are large and comfortable-looking mansions, sur-rounded by well-fenced farms, though it is evident that some of these are not in a very flourishing condition. We were told that the old tars were too liberal in the rites of hospitality to get rich, and that after having plowed the ocean so long, they did not take kindly with plowing the prairie.

Here, as in other parts of the West, there are no inns except in the towns, or on the most frequented routes, consequently the traveller must shift in the best way he can, and when in want of food for himself or his horse, must request all such accommodation as a favour, besides paying for it. We very seldom found much difficulty, however, in getting either food or lodging, such as it was; but when an instance did occur, in which we were refused admittance, we took the thing calmly, and jogged on with the best grace we might. Just as we were about to leave the Marine Settlement, we rode up to a house, and on arriving at the fence, which is generally found either surrounding the house or enclosing a small space on its front, we saw the owner reclining in the shade of the stoop, with his chair tilted on its hind legs, and his feet deposited on the table. On our asking if he would let us have some food for our horses, he replied "no." As the day was very hot, and we were thirsty, we asked if we might come over to his well and draw some water, and on his saying "yes," we hitched our horses to the fence, and drew up a bucket of water. Not another word passed, except a question about the quality of some apples which lay near, and to which he replied shortly, but quite civilly. It was evident that he did not want to be troubled with us, but it was quite as evident that he meant nothing disrespectful, and we should have been very foolish if we had felt annoyed at his conduct.

After travelling a mile or two, we made another application at a house on the way-side, where we were more successful; and after watering and getting some food for our horses, we entered the house, which was neat and comfortable. The boarded walls of the room into which we were introduced, were furnished with some indifferent prints, and some samples of needlework, which latter we judged were wrought by two young women, the daughters of our hostess. The lady of the house was tidily dressed, and appeared more buxom, and was less reserved in her manner, than the generality of females in that part of the country. After adroitly manœuvring till she found out where we were from, she complimented us by giving us the history of her fortunes, and to do her justice, it must be said that she had very few *mis*fortunes to complain of. She told us that she had come from Pennsylvania, that her husband was a blacksmith, and that he wrought at his trade and cultivated some land which he had purchased. When tired of speaking of her own affairs, she gave us the history of some of her neighbours, and chatted away with great good humour, without appearing concerned about anything under the sun; but an eclipse of that luminary, which, she had been informed, was to take place in a day or two, caused her some anxious thoughts, and she did not well know what to make of it. She had been told, she said, by some very good people, that such things brought bad luck, and that they were always followed by war, pestilence, or some disaster. To be sure sickness had been mighty bad that season, but then it had begun before the *clip*. She went on to say, that as the clip was to be total, as they called it, who could tell if the sun would ever come back again; their doctor, who was a mighty smart man, and knew 'most anything, had laughed at her, and said all such stories were nonsense. Finally, she asked our serious opinion on the subject, and seemed glad when we told her that we agreed with the doctor.

We got a most capital dinner, for in the kindness of her heart our hostess seemed to have ransacked her whole larder; and we sat down to a table literally encumbered with dishes. The whole charge was 25 cents. each.

On travelling by the more frequented tracts, and where inns and houses of entertainment are rare, the farmers by the way seldom refuse to entertain and lodge travellers; though many of them, I am aware, would much rather not be troubled in that way, for, though they do in self-defence make a charge, yet their accommodation is often but scanty, and they are put to very considerable inconvenience.

A few miles further on we entered on a branch of Looking-glass prairie, Bond county, where long reaches of green undulating prairie stretched away till they became lost in the haze of distance; and, within a few hours of sunset, we emerged from a grove on the shore of one which lay stretched out before us like an ocean. In the direction which the track we were following took, we could just distinguish the forest like a low bank of cloud, whilst on our right the prairie stretched away, one vast plain, uninterrupted by tree or bush, as far as the eye could reach. The prospect, though grand, was by no means encouraging, as it was evident that all the speed we could muster would be barely sufficient to ensure our crossing before dark.

We entered on the track at our best pace, and yet, for a considerable time, the dark stripe of forest appeared as indistinct as when we commenced. The solitude of the forest is not half so oppressive as that of the ocean-like prairie. There is variety, and one can always find something to admire in the forest; one can hold converse with the monarchs of ages, whose limbs have shadowed the red man long before the "pale faces" came to drive him from the land of his fathers; one can admire the deer as he bounds away, or the stately turkey, with his beautiful and varying plumage, as he darts off with the speed of a hound; there is the lively squirrel, too, and, should the time be spring, that prince of songsters, the ferruginous thrush; though he, as if unwilling to throw his music away on the unpeopled wilderness, is most frequently heard near some settlement; above all, one cannot see half a day's journey before him (except in some instances where lines have been cut for roads), and is always in hope of something, however trifling, occurring to beguile the way; whereas, the middle of one of these large prairies is a perfect solitude, without a living thing, except such as one would much rather want than have, viz., greenhead flies in thousands, snakes basking on the dusty track, and myriads of grasshoppers, some of them as large as the little finger, darting through the air like arrows, and sometimes coming full tilt against the face.

We had for some time seen, in the direction we were travelling, what we hoped from its appearance was a column of smoke, though we had some suspicion that it might turn out a cloud of dust raised by some traveller. It brought us in mind of the smoke of a steamer seen at sea, when the vessel is below the horizon; and some time passed before we became fully aware that it was dust, raised by something coming towards us; and, by and bye, we could see a person on horseback, with whom we finally met about the middle of the prairie.

Travellers, when they meet in the wilder districts, mostly stop and chat for a short time, as each can give to the other some information about the route he has come. In this instance, we enquired the distance to the nearest place where it was likely we should be able to procure a night's lodging, with a description of the route to it. He told us there was situated on the margin of the woods which we were nearing, a house where he thought we might " get to stay." Having got a minute description of the house and its locality, we resumed our journey.

The people in the backwoods are capital at giving directions to a traveller for the route he is to follow; not the slightest peculiarity in the surface of the ground, not an old log, or singular-looking tree, is omitted. The patience of the narrator seems to be inexhaustible; and he will go over and over the items, till the person receiving the information is satisfied. The very children take a world of pains to direct a traveller. I never had any difficulty in finding my way after such instructions, except in one instance, and then my informant was a Dutchman, who sent me right into a marsh, from which I had some difficulty in extricating myself.

The track across the prairie seemed as interminable as Paddy's rope, from which, he swore, some one had cut off the other end altogether; and the sun went down, and the shadows of

evening began to deepen, whilst we were still at some distance from the woods. As the time between sunset and dark
in these latitudes is short, we urged on our weary horses, and
were fortunate enough to pilot our way to the house we had
been directed to, just as night was setting in. We hallooed at the
fence, when a woman came to the door, who, on our asking if we
might be allowed to stay all night, replied " yes," and returned
into the house.

We commenced a search for the well, which we soon found;
but the water was so bad, that our horses, although they had
travelled many hours in a hot sun, would not taste it. On examining the water by daylight, it looked like tea slightly coloured
with cream, and had a rank disagreeable smell. The farmer's
hogs were less fastidious than our horses, and waited with
great impatience till we left, when a dreadful conflict ensued
about the rude trough, hewed with an axe out of the trunk
of a tree, into which we had poured some of the water. Some
one cried to us to " cover in the well with the boards again that
the hogs mightn't jump in"—it appeared to be about thirty feet
deep. In order to preserve the water in a state of purity, it is
necessary to have the mouth of the well shut in with boards,
either laid flat over it, with a hatch in them; or to surround it to
a height sufficient to prevent animals and reptiles from getting
in. Rabbits and snakes are the most common intruders.

Having unsaddled our horses and rummaged about till we got
corn and fodder for them, we entered the house, which was comparatively a good one, built of brick, and of two stories. The
inmates consisted of the woman who had so laconically given us
permission to stay, and two young men, with two females, evidently visitors; there were also two children, but whether they
belonged to the house, to the visitors, or to some absent persons,
I do not think I fairly concluded upon, as they seemed to act
independently of all parties.

During the short time we sat, before and after supper, there
were scarcely half a dozen words of conversation, an occurrence
quite characteristic of the people, when the sexes are met. The
silence of the woods is not half so oppressive, a pin can't fall
without being heard, and the jaws of those who yawn through
sheer weariness, are heard cracking right and left. The men
generally are not very talkative; but I believe the women are
much like women all the world over, and I have in some instances
overheard them unfasten the sluices of their eloquence, and
fairly maintain the character of their sex.

Next morning we had some conversation with the young men

and a brother-in-law of theirs, who had come from his farm, which was at no great distance. They shewed us a patent plough, which the young men's father had invented, and it was by far the handsomest and most efficient looking plough that I had yet seen in the country.

The orchard here was beautiful, and contained some hundreds of trees, all engrafted, and of choice kinds, and I do not think I ever saw or tasted finer apples. We were told that some orchards in this neighbourhood contained one thousand bearing trees, whose fruit afforded some hundreds of barrels of cider. Apple trees grow with great rapidity, and get to a large size in not many years. Coal had been found in this neighbourhood, but not in great plenty. The land is very good, but far from markets or boatable waters.

Advancing east the prairies continue very fine, and of great extent; at intervals, cut by meandering groves into insulated portions of great beauty, and frequently varied by scattered clumps of trees, like islands in a lake.

Passing through the small town of Greenville, we arrived at Vandalia, then the capital of the state of Illinois.* This town is situated on the west bank of the Kaskaskia, or Okau (as it is called further down), on an elevated ridge overhanging the river; it is a scattered place, with some good buildings, and a large open space in the centre for a square.

Bilious fever prevailed here, and there were several patients in the hotel where we stayed.

The country here, adjoining the Kaskaskia, is heavily timbered, and there is a very extensive morass on the river bottom opposite the town.

We here struck the National Road, which comes, or rather is to come, in a tolerably direct line from Wheeling, on the Ohio, by Columbus, Springfield (O.), Indianapolis, Terre Haute, and, after leaving Vandalia, is to run to Alton on the Mississippi.— Most part of this road is nothing more than a track, though, I believe, the line has been surveyed, and the timber cut down and removed, the stumps being left. Several miles of the road to the east of Vandalia had been formed, and some of it completed across the swamp, which must otherwise have been nearly impassable. The huge ditches, from which the earth had been taken to raise the road, were in many places full of water, and yet the season had been singularly dry, and the river had scarcely ever been seen so low. Vandalia cannot be a healthy place with this

---

* By an act of the state legislature, the seat of government was to be removed from this place to Springfield, in Sangamon, in 1840.

dismal swamp on the one side, and some very low wet prairies on the other.

On leaving the swamp and the woods we passed a number of labourers forming the road on the prairie; this was done by merely excavating the earth from each side, and throwing it into the middle, without any covering of stones, and, owing to the dryness of the climate, such roads will stand a great deal of passage. When they become rutted, or broken, they are levelled with the plough.

The greenhead flies were so numerous here, that we had to carry branches and keep up a constant warfare with them. The season for them was rather past, which was fortunate, as, in all likelihood, we should have been obliged to have travelled over the prairies during the night, a plan sometimes resorted to.

At Cumberland, a small, wretched-looking place, we stopped to get some water and corn for our horses. We happened to apply at the house of a person who figured as doctor, but whose right to that title was anything but doubtful. The water in the doctor's well was execrable, and if he only could have induced people to come and drink of it, he need never have wanted patients. Some of his own family were on the sick list. The doctor was called away a few minutes after we entered the house, when his wife, who was recovering from fever, began and praised him to the skies. She did not attempt to conceal that he had no diploma, but then he was so smart, besides she was herself the daughter of one who had practised the healing art, and she somehow made it appear that this circumstance ought to have very considerable weight in forming an estimate of her husband's qualifications. She was like Sancho, when he said it was quite natural for him to be a good judge of wine, for he had two relations by the father's side that were the nicest tasters in La Mancha.

There was, lying on a table, a well-thumbed copy of an early edition of Graham's Domestic Medicine, printed at London.

On this the first day of our travel on the National Road, we met several parties of movers, i. e. emigrants, travelling west, and we continued to meet them daily, and often in large numbers, so long as we travelled on this line of road, which we did to Columbus in Ohio. This current of emigration sets steadily to the westward, during the whole summer and fall, winter frequently overtaking some of the parties before they arrive at their intended destination. When this is the case, they winter in the best way they can, and, it sometimes happens, that they take a liking to the place and move no further. A very large proportion of those we met were going to Missouri, but to what spot in the state few of them could precisely say.

This wandering life possesses such charms for many, that they never remain very many years in one place; but, after having partially improved a farm, and put up some *fixings,* sell off, hitch the horses to the waggon, and, driving their stock along with them, again move to the outskirts of civilization.

This taste for moving and living in the wilderness seems strange to the denizen of an *old* country, but habit, which binds him to the home of his forefathers, is no less powerful in modifying the feelings of the pioneer of the woods, and it would be as uncongenial for the one to live in the crowded city as for the other to live miles from the sight of any smoke but that which arose from his own hearth.

When travelling through a thinly-peopled part of Illinois, an anecdote was related to us of one of these frontier settlers, which is very characteristic. A person, an acquaintance of our informant, and who knew the settler referred to, happening to pass his log hut one day, called on him. On asking him how he was getting along, he shook his head and replied, " Well, I can't tell, I think I'll move." " Move, why?" " Well, the country is getting so peopled up I can't live in it no how." — " Why, the last time I saw you, you told me your next neighbour lived seven miles off." " Yes, but there is one within three miles now, and I can't stand it no longer; one can't go out into the woods but he hears the sound of the axe and the crash of trees."

Such settlers as the one here alluded to are mostly squatters, and run the risk of being turned out by any person purchasing the land; but, where land is so plenty, few will incur the odium attached to ousting a man from such a possession, without at least giving him the value of the improvements, i. e. houses, fences, and broken-up prairie, which he may have made upon it.

Towards evening we arrived at Ewington, on the Little Wabash river, and by the advice of a person with whom we fell in by the way, we passed through it, to take our chance of getting a night's lodging at a " squire's" about a mile beyond.

Ewington is a sorry-looking place, situated on a high clay bank of the Little Wabash, which is here an inconsiderable stream, deeply cut into the surface of the country, and jammed full of driftwood. It would have been quite impassable at this place for horses, had it not been for a primitive and ricketty wood bridge, erected across the chasm.

Before we got to the squire's abode, the night was as dark as pitch, and as the road was full of ruts and other impediments, our progress was very slow. A horse with the use of his eyes will seldom tumble into a hole, however dark the night may be; but, in going among trees, he estimates the practicability of a passage between the trunks, or below limbs, merely in reference to his own bulk, without taking into account the legs or body of his rider; so that the knees sometimes get awkward thumps, and there is some risk of being swept off by a branch.

The squire was unwilling to admit us, saying he had two guests already, which were as many as he had beds for; besides, his old woman was sick, and could not again be troubled with preparing supper. In reply to these objections, we told him that we would sit by the fire, or lie on the floor, and would not trouble the old woman with making any supper. In the end he relented and took us in; and, though we did lie on the floor, the old woman was kind enough of her own accord to relieve us of the additional penalty of being supperless.

The squire was an intelligent man; his forte, however, seemed to be the mechanism of mills, and he detailed to us several projected improvements in saw mills. The Americans are decidedly a mechanical people—a people of shifts and expedients, which may be the offspring of that fruitful mother of invention, necessity.

Of the other two strangers, one was the driver of the stage between Vandalia and Terre Haute; no sinecure on such detestable roads. There had been an overturn of the stage that very day, and at the time it took place the driver was slowly leading the horses by the heads, whilst another person was doing his best, by pulling at the upper side, to keep the vehicle on its wheels. The driver spoke of the affair as a good joke.

We left the squire's at sunrise next morning, and through the day travelled over some extensive prairies. The population was very thin, and the grass was growing rank and tall in many places, without a single trail in it. Snakes were abundant, and, judging from the trails of these reptiles on the dusty track, some of them must have been large.

The groves on these unpeopled prairies, are not fringed by a growth of young wood and bushes, as they are where the country is more thickly settled, and where the fire has been kept out for a few years; but, on the contrary, rise up abruptly from the grassy margin, hemming it in as with a wall. Wild turkey were very plentiful, and we saw flocks running off the tracks into the woods.

The river Embarras, as it name implies, would be a troublesome impediment to the first explorers of the country, as it is a sluggish stream, apt to get deeply flooded, and is bounded by lofty clay banks; now, however, a good wooden bridge, and an elevated roadway across the bottom, secure an easy passage.

About an hour before sunset, we met two men on horseback, in the middle of a prairie. It turned out that, like us, they were strangers to this part of the country, and were on the outlook for a favourable situation in which to locate. They told us they had been up the Wabash, but did not like the country, it was so sickly, and that sickness prevailed wherever they had been. We gave them such information as we could about the country we had come through, but could give them very little encouragement respecting its present healthiness. Before parting, mutual enquiries were made respecting the chance of getting lodgings for the night, when we directed them to an embryo town at no great distance, and they told us of a house, the only one for a long way on the road. At this house, situated at the bottom of a deep valley among the woods, we arrived a short time before dark, and were told we might stay if we could put up with such accommodation as the inmates could afford. The two travellers we met on the road had given us no very favourable account of the place, and it did look very wretched; but there was no alternative, except sleeping in the woods, and the nights had become too cool to make that agreeable. The family consisted of a man and his wife, with five or six young folks, and every one in the house was either lying in fever, or just recovering from it. We were in "pretty considerable of a bad fix," but had roughed it too long now to be dismayed, and so set to work to kindle a fire in an unoccupied and totally unfurnished end of the loghouse, where we speculated on remaining through the night. We had just fanned the logs into a cheerful blaze, when there arrived an inundation of movers, which crowded the house full of men, women, and children. This might be called the *coup de grace* to our hopes of getting any rest. Our supper consisted of rancid bacon, coffee burnt as black as charcoal, and Indian bread compounded with the dripping of the bacon. That fever patients ever recovered under such a regimen, "how it cam, let doctors tell."

The names of the young people in this family had certainly been culled from some of the old romances, and I could scarcely retain my gravity when the "old woman" addressed a tall, sickly, squalid-looking boy, by the name of Altamont. I have forgotten the names of some of the others, but they were of the same class.

As we had come first, we had the precedence, and were honoured with the only spare bed in the house, whilst the floor was completely occupied by the movers. I lay down with my clothes on, but what with the moaning of a poor girl who was lying in fever, and the screaming of a restless child, to sleep was out of the question, and in a short time I arose with the intention of going out a little. The folks on the floor had made their arrangements in the dark, so I did not know how they were situated, and my first step was made at a venture. I scarcely could have been less fortunate, as I stepped plump on the child which had already created so much disturbance, but which had become quiet for a few minutes, and in making an exertion to save it, got into fresh difficulties of a somewhat delicate nature, and finally was glad to make my escape on all fours.

We started next morning, the 9th September, at break of day. There had been a sharp frost through the night, and as the season had hitherto been very warm, we were glad to add to our thin clothing by putting on our cloaks.

On passing a house newly built, we had to avoid a deep hole dug right in the middle of the road (the State Road, be it remembered), from which the clay for daubing the chimney had evidently been taken. To be sure the road was a mere track, but there was a good deal of passage on it, and it was the route of a stage carrying the mail. The State Roads, being under the controul of the state legislatures, are generally exempt from such annoyances as this; but with the other roads of the country, every one interferes when it suits his convenience, and there is nothing uncommon in coming up to a fence which has been thrown across the road, thereby causing the traveller to make a detour in order to regain the track. In some places, where the country is getting peopled up, the roads are flung about from one farm to another, in a manner perfectly vexatious and perplexing. This evil, which might very easily be remedied now, will soon become a source of trouble and expence. Such a go-a-head people as the Americans will not long endure to be kept tacking through the country like Commodore Trunion.

During the day, we stopped at a house on the roadside to get some refreshment, and whilst it was being prepared, a man entered the house to make enquiry if our host was going to attend a trial before the judge, to which it appeared both had been cited, whether as witnesses or principals I did not learn. After a good deal of swearing, they came to the conclusion that they would not go; they did not care for either judge or laws. Whilst they were discussing this point, the stranger drew from his pocket a bottle of whisky, which he handed, first to the lady of the house, who put it to her head and took a good pull, and then to her husband.   As before stated, the people on the thoroughfares do not constitute a fair sample of the mass.

In the afternoon we arrived at Marshall, a new town, situated on a small rising prairie, at the intersection of the National Road with that leading from Chicàgo, on Lake Michigan, by Danville and Paris, to Vincennes, on the Wabash, and thence to Louisville, on the Ohio.   Although this place was quite new, a great number of lots had been sold, and already partially built upon, and there was one continued bustle of hewing, hammering, and sawing going on.

The place is beautifully situated, and from the impetus already given to it, is likely to become of some importance.   The Wabash, the nearest boatable water, is six or eight miles off.

At several places in this neighbourhood, large gangs of labourers were working at the National Road, cutting and embanking at some deep ravines, and some stone piers for bridges were being erected, the materials for which were cut in large masses from a compact limestone, approaching in appearance to marble.   Among the labourers, there was no mistaking some of the *pisantry*, and Pat's joke and loud laugh startled the echos of the western woods.

The face of the country here began to assume a different appearance, and at Marshall we left the last prairie, with the exception of a small one at Terre Haute on the Wabash bottom, and which, probably, is of comparatively recent formation.   The woods partook of the change too, and the oak was frequently supplanted by the beech, and we here first fell in with the tulip tree, or poplar as it is sometimes called.

Leaving Marshall, we travelled through beech woods till we came to the Wabash bottom, which we reached at dusk.   The bottom was heavily timbered, and a dismal swampy looking place, and it proved quite as bad as it looked.   The track was tortuous and narrow, interrupted with stumps and huge gnarled roots, with, now and then, an apology for a bridge, consisting of two trees laid for bearers, crossed at right angles by split rails, laid on *en corduroy*, and unfastened, except by a rail laid over their extremities and pinned down at each end, and which, of course, prevented the rails when firmly packed from getting asunder, but allowed them to roll and clatter in such a way as to render the passage very insecure and unpleasant.   We had no time, however, to pick our steps, for the woods looked more sombre, and the slimy pools more inky every moment, and be-

z

fore we were half way across the bottom the darkness was intense, and we were brought to our slowest pace. We knew that we must soon strike the river, and were under some apprehension that we might ride into it over head and ears before we were aware, an apprehension not entirely groundless, as our horses, like most of those in the West, would have entered the Father of waters himself without the slightest token of uneasiness.

The lights of Terre Haute, at no great distance, indicated our near approach to the river, of whose placid surface we caught the glimmer when within a few yards of the perpendicular clay bank, within which its waters, when low, are here confined. Uncertain where the ferry might be, I left my horse in charge of my friend, and groped about until I came against a rail fence, and thought I could distinguish a house between me and the sky, and abruptly came in view of a stream of light issuing from an open door. On enquiring of two men, whom I found within, where the ferry was, neither of them made me any answer, but, on my repeating my request for information, one of them started to his feet in a rage, and uttering a volley of oaths, swore he would ferry no more that night, that it was quite enough to work through the day, without being called upon every hour in the night, as they had been of late, by the doctors, and by people seeking them for the sick. I sympathized with him, saying it was very hard indeed. "Why did'nt you stay on the other side of the bottom?" said he. "You won't give over coming through that ere dark bottom till you get murdered. It was only the other night that one got himself skivered between this and Paris. I would'nt pass through that bottom after sundown for fifty dollars." I told him that we were strangers, unacquainted with the country, and finally prevailed upon them to take us across. We found a very good inn, and, although the hour was past, experienced no difficulty in procuring supper.

Terre Haute (*Terry Hut* as the name is universally pronounced), in the state of Indiana, is situated on a gently rising eminence on the east side of the Wabash, and is a pretty place, with a number of good houses, and some respectable stores and inns. One of the stores, an extensive hardware concern, was the property of Messrs. McGregor and Rae, two Scotchmen, on whom we took the liberty of calling. Mr. McGregor received us very kindly, but we did not see Mr. Rae, who was confined to his room by sickness. Some of the inmates of the hotel where we stopped, were lying dangerously ill in fever.

The Wabash is not, I believe, at all times navigable for steamers above the rapids near White river, a short way below

Vincennes, and somewhat over one hundred miles below Terre Haute, but, when the water is high, steamers ascend to Lafayette, Indiana, a distance of 124 miles above Terre Haute, and of 346 from the Ohio. No doubt a canal will ere long be cut to remedy the obstruction at the rapids.

We left Terre Haute after breakfast, and crossed a fine cultivated bottom of considerable extent, lying between the town and the ancient bluff of the river. Numbers of workmen were busy on the National Road, raising it above the surface level of the bottom, and covering it with a thick layer of well-broken limestone. The bottom which, here and at some other places on this river, partakes of the character of prairie, seemed to be subject to inundation.

The bluff, and the country for some way towards the east, consists of a pale red, friable sandstone, which becomes rounded when exposed to the action of the atmosphere, and is very like our new red sandstone.

The stream of movers was still flowing west with unabated numbers, and, this day, we met, amongst others, with a troop consisting of a number of families of Mormonites, with all their household goods, horses, cattle, sheep, &c., bound to some place in Missouri, where there is a settlement consisting entirely of that sect of religionists.

The country here is heavily timbered, and, among other fine trees, we saw some enormous poplars (tulip tree). The poplar, when old, is one of the most ungainly of forest trees. It rises to a great height without a limb, carrying its thickness, slightly diminished, nearly to the top, where it abruptly terminates with a scant and ungraceful foliage. We never saw one with a straight stem, but, on the contrary, all are more or less awkwardly twisted.

When practicable, the National Road runs in a straight line, which circumstance, when the country is level, renders travelling exceedingly monotonous. Hemmed in by a wall of forest the traveller can sometimes see a distance of many miles before him the cleared roadway diminished to a thread-like tenuity. Inns and villages, however, occur at no great distance from one another, so that the traveller on horseback or on foot has it in his power to halt and get rest and food when he requires them; and the accommodation is better than it is farther west. The houses standing back from the line of road, of course, cannot be seen until one is close upon them, but the owners of the inns take care to intimate their whereabouts, by erecting within view, huge signs, which can be discerned a long way. Washington, mostly

z 2

in some questionable shape, like the transmuted head of Sir Roger de Coverly, figures largely on those *chefs d'oeuvres*. The patriot commonly stands, his eyes fixt on vacancy, with a cocked hat in one hand, whilst the other has possession of a tumbler, into which some liquor, after performing the singular feat of leaping out of a jug into the air, is falling in a manner quite in keeping with the rest of the performance. The jug is held by a lady dressed in black shoes, white stockings, and printed cotton gown, with a broad ribbon round the waist, her face as white as chalk, and her eyes as black as coal, and with an expression indicating her total unconsciousness of what she is about, or in whose presence she stands; a dereliction which it is possible may have excited the ale to such an unwonted act of courtesy. The sign-board, however large it might be, never in any instance contained in one line the name of the owner, one or two letters at the end of the name being put over the others in a reduced size, and this was evidently the fashion. We saw the origin of this fashion in the West, where the keeper of a grocery or a *hotel* does his own sign painting with his finger or a bit of stick dipt among pounded charcoal and water, when, like a schoolboy commencing the art of caligraphy, the operator mostly attains the end of the line before the word is completed.

In the evening we arrived at Manhattan, a small and recent place, and, of two inns, had the good fortune to choose that kept by a Mr. Harris, originally from the state of New York. Mr. Harris was a squire (similar to our justice of the peace), a distinction, the result no doubt of his intelligence.

When going to start next morning, we found both our horses so lame as to render it quite impracticable to proceed with them : they were leg-weary and cramped with travel. Such an accident could not have befallen us in better quarters, and, otherwise, it was quite as well that we did not proceed, as the sky began to lower, and it commenced raining heavily early in the forenoon ; the first rain that had fallen at Manhattan for fifteen weeks.

During the day, some more travellers were brought up by the state of the weather, and before night we had a considerable, and somewhat miscellaneous, party round a roaring wood fire. The most interesting among the strangers was an old gentleman of the name of Bryant, who had been intimately acquainted with the celebrated Daniel Boon, who had lived sometime in his fathers' family and had married one of his cousins. When Boon penetrated into the interior of Kentucky, Bryant formed one of thirty who accompanied him to make a settlement. Bryant, when we saw him, was still a cheerful, healthy old man, telling with great zest many good hunting stories and feats in Indian warfare, and spoke of *hunting Injuns* as if they had been bears or panthers. When narrating an Indian skirmish, he would get up, and, stalking stealthily about from place to place, with a stick for a rifle, which was always on the " make ready," with the thumb of the right hand working away about the place where the dog-head should have been, would bite his lip and fix his eye in the direction of his imaginary foe, sometimes suddenly jerking up the stick and letting it fall again as if defeated in his intention of firing, and then he would stretch himself up behind a tree (there was a wooden pillar quite convenient), looking eagerly on all sides. He was kind enough to favour us with a great deal of advice with regard to Indian hunting, which I am afraid was sadly thrown away upon us.

Squire Harris had one of the huge signs already mentioned, with a somewhat confused representation upon it of, what we conceived to be, the American eagle in the act of throttling the English lion. It is possible, however, that we might be wrong in our solution of the hieroglyphic, and Mr. Harris seemed unaccountably unwilling to enlighten us on the subject, and to the question of a neighbour, who in our presence asked when " he was going to pull down that ere sign," the squire replied by authoritatively bidding him hold his tongue.

There is some coal and excellent limestone in this neighbourhood, the latter being cut in large blocks and dressed for the works on the National Road.

After staying two days at Manhattan, we resumed our journey. The country in this neighbourhood is cut into inequalities by numerous creeks and branches, which render it more interesting than the flatter districts; the timber is splendid, and the foliage was beginning to assume some of the autumnal tints, in consequence of two or three nights of sharp frost.

A few miles to the east of Manhattan, we first fell in with those boulders which are found scattered over such a large extent of the surface of the North American continent. As the change is somewhat sudden and pretty well defined, there is reason to believe that the current, which undoubtedly has deposited these remains, either found a shore here, or some obstruction which arose above the general level of the bottom of the sea, and which prevented the boulders from being carried farther in a westerly direction. The prairies commence a short way to the west of this, and the deposit which forms their basis, so far as I ever saw, with the exception of a few solitary stones, contains nothing larger than small pebbles

The red sandstone, before mentioned, intervenes between this and the valley of the Wabash, which at Terre Haute, bounds the prairie on the east, and this sandstone appeared more elevated than either the prairie or that part of the country where the boulders commenced; I may mention too that the boulders were not so large, nor apparently so unequal in size, here as they were farther east. They consisted principally of granite.

At Manhattan we had met with a traveller who was going east, and whom we again passed on the road. As the weather had become showery some covering to exclude the rain had become a desideratum, and our traveller had assumed one which had at least the merit of novelty—a half hide of leather. He said he had not been able to procure an umbrella, that he had a use for the leather when he should get to the end of his journey, and that, in the meantime, it answered the purpose just as well as anything else. A Yankee is commonly fertile in expedients; his resources, in emergency, have not been narrowed by the system of division of labour which chains a man's mind to a single department of one art.

Indianapolis, the capital of the state of Indiana, is situated on White River. The Capitol, or State House, on the model of the Parthenon, is finely situated in a large open space, and has a very imposing appearance. True it is built only of brick and stucco, which is painted in imitation of stone, still it is large and well proportioned, and forms a pleasing object.

A canal was being cut from this to the Ohio. The country is getting quickly peopled up, and the land is of good quality. The city has some very good hotels, stores, &c., with a population of about 2,000. Fever was very prevalent, and there had been many deaths.

We here found it necessary to dispose of our horses, as we were desirous of proceeding faster than we had hitherto done. On making enquiry, we found that the most common method of sale was by auction, and having engaged an auctioneer, we put our horses into his hands. He mounted one of them and commenced perambulating the place, calling out that the horse was for sale, and, on getting an offer, intimated the sum in the ordinary way. In this manner he proceeded till no more offers were to be had, when he came and reported to us. In this manner we disposed of them both, including saddles and bridles.

Early next morning we started by stage for Centreville. It was a hard frost, with a dreadfully keen wind, scarcely endurable by us who had so recently been broiling in a temperature, which, for many weeks, ranged from 90° to 100° in the shade. The land generally seemed good, and was heavily timbered. The population was very considerable.

The National Road was still, in many places, no more than a track winding its way among boulders and the stumps of the trees which had been cut on surveying the line, but the horses are good and the drivers are fearless, and dash on through thick and thin, very much at the expense of the poor passengers' bones. During the day, we came to a small stream with a marshy bottom or flat at one side, across which were a most insufficient bridge and corduroy road. Our approach to this *fixing* being by a very steep bank down which we rattled at a slapping pace, we had almost run foul of a poor fellow's waggon, which had got stuck fast with one wheel in the marsh. In trying to avoid Scylla, in the shape of a hole in the corduroy, he had got into Charybdis. After having laid a few rotten sticks on the hole, the driver mounted the box, and starting at a rapid pace, cleared all difficulties, the passengers crossing on foot.

At dusk we arrived at Centreville, on White Water River, which here runs against a high bluff, along whose face, of perpendicular rock, a road was being cut as an approach to a wooden bridge which had been thrown across the river. Although the track was still very narrow, and dangerous, from the risk of being precipitated into the river, still the folks of this go-a-head country could not wait till it was finished, but must needs force their way amongst fragments of rock, which the numerous workmen were blasting and splitting, and a score of carts, which were leading away the earth and stones.

Centreville is situated in a fine country tolerably well cleared and thickly peopled. The farm houses are comfortable, in many instances with fine orchards attached to them, and not the slightest symptom of poverty or want is to be seen. Some of the small rivers in the district are beautiful, clear streams, running over gravelly beds.

We left Centreville before daylight, and, at Richmond, struck off to the right of the line of the National Road, which was here rendered impassable by some improvements in the course of being made upon it. A short way from Richmond we passed into the state of Ohio. The country continued fine and was more diversified with, not exactly, hill and dale, but with greater inequalities of surface than many parts we had lately seen, and was more or less covered with gravel, and boulders of limestone and granite, some of these containing, perhaps, 40 or 50 cubic feet.

About mid-day we arrived at Dayton, the prettiest and most flourishing place we had yet seen in our journey east. The town is finely situated on an extensive bottom on the River Miami, and is surrounded by a very fine country. The streets are wide, with handsome brick buildings, large and well furnished stores, and capacious hotels; many of the luxuries of the most civilized countries have an abiding place in Dayton. There are several mills and factories, and a large building, intended for a cotton factory, was nearly finished when we passed. The town is connected with the Ohio at Cincinnati, by the Miami canal, which is about 66 miles in length: land in the neighbourhood from 20 to 50 dollars an acre.

We spent a few hours waiting for the stage to Springfield. The hotel in which we were was very large and crowded, indeed few objects in the country are more surprising to the stranger, than these establishments, which, at first sight, often appear so disproportioned to the other accessaries. When the stage arrived, it was found that the passengers for Springfield were too numerous for one conveyance, there was no difficulty, however, as another stage was speedily provided, and off the two started on the National Road, which, though macadamized in some parts, was very bad in others. Numbers of labourers were at work at different points on the road to Springfield, at which place we arrived sometime after dark. In a few hours we continued our route for Columbus, and day broke whilst we were on the road, which was now excellent. The land here appeared not so good as that in the neighbourhood of Dayton. There were some merino sheep and short horned cattle, and several herds of mules; some of them consisting of 50 or 100 of these animals. The tide of movers was still flowing west.

Columbus, the capital of the state of Ohio, is situated on the Scioto river, and a few miles from the Ohio Canal. This canal traverses the entire extent of the state, from Cleveland on Lake Erie in the north, to Portsmouth on the Ohio in the south, and is 310 miles in length. There is a branch canal from the main trunk to Columbus, which place is distant from Cleveland, by canal, about 200 miles, and 139 by stage. There is a fine penitentiary, with several churches and good hotels. The bottoms on the Scioto are extensive and very fertile, but very little of the cleared land in the neighbourhood is yet free from stumps.

We took stage from Columbus to Sandusky City on Lake Erie. One of the passengers, a person from New Orleans, was one of the most ruffianly swearers I ever heard, and I very much doubt if poor uncle Toby's army in Flanders swore half so terribly. Another was a vender of base coin. The third, most fortunately, was a very intelligent and agreeable gentleman.

Without the occurrence of anything extraordinary, with the exception of the swearing of the *gentleman* from New Orleans, we proceeded till the day was pretty far advanced, when some one made enquiry about the place at which we were to dine, and which was found still to be many miles distant, and that owing to the stage having had to wait at Columbus, some hours over time for the mails, we should not arrive till the evening. This state of affairs was by no means satisfactory, and the passengers unanimously determined to insist upon the stage stopping at the first place at which dinner could be procured ; and we did stop, the driver making no objection.

There is some prairie between Marion and Bucyrus some of which appeared to be good. We noticed a few flocks of sheep grazing on it. Here I for the first time saw the black squirrel ; there was no such thing in any part of the West that I had visited.

At Bucyrus, and some other places in this district, there are mineral springs ; those at Bucyrus being, I believe, what are commonly called sulphur springs.

For a considerable distance to the north of Bucyrus, the country is very level, newly settled, and covered with a forest of heavy timber. The road, often very bad, was rendered tedious by its straightness and uniformity. Prairie, very flat, with granite and limestone boulders in great quantity, occurs again before arriving at the ridge, or ancient shore of lake Erie. The ridge, at this point, is not, like the more famous one between Lockport and Rochester, composed of gravel, but is a precipitous bank, consisting of a coarse limestone, and, after directing the eye along its sinuosities, and over the marshy flat which extends from its base, one cannot doubt that the waters of lake Erie have at some period reached it. The distance from this point to the lake at Sandusky, is 12 or 14 miles. The plain is in some places completely covered with boulders, embedded in a black mud-like loam ; and, about half-way across, there occurs a stripe of deep loose sand, where the plain makes another descent, and where, it is possible, there may have been another shore. The difference between the present level of the lake and that of the first ridge, must be very considerable.

We arrived at Sandusky about sunset on the second evening after leaving Columbus. It was quite refreshing to hear the beating of the surf, and to inhale the breeze which fanned the

bosom of this inland sea. There was something like the glad-
ness of recognition, in the dancing of the waves; which seemed
to welcome us like old friends.

Sandusky is a small place, and is one of the ports of call for the
steamers on their way up and down the lake. It is distant from
Buffalo 247 miles, and 70 miles from Detroit.

We were aroused from our beds in the night, and hurried
aboard a steamer crowded with passengers. In the cabin there
was not room even to sit, much less to lie down, so that we, along
with a number of others, had to wander about like so many ghosts.
In the fore part of the cabin there was a large dais covered with
green cloth, which was occupied by as many as it could hold
wedged close together; and all the chairs, tables, and benches
were clad. The night air off the lake was very cold; but more
endurable than the stew in the cabin. Before daylight we put
into Huron, a small place at the mouth of the river of that
name; and did not leave till about noon, as the captain of the
boat had a daughter in the place to be married that day. The
passengers, of course, had nothing for it but to suffer the injustice of such delay with what patience they might. The perfect
indifference to the interests and comfort of passengers, displayed
by the captains of steamboats, on the rivers and lakes here, cannot
fail to be impressed on a native of the old country, and to make
him feel that matters are, as yet, as well managed at home. I
am not aware, however, that the captains of the lake steamers
are so blameable on this account, as those of the western rivers.

Going down the lake, we touched at several ports; the principal of which were Cleveland, and Erie; the former a place of
very considerable trade, with the advantage of being situated at
the terminus of the Ohio Canal. After a hard contested race
with another steamer we arrived at Buffalo.

Buffalo, situated at the eastern extremity of Lake Erie, and
at the terminus of the Erie Canal, is, in all probability, destined
to become a great place, as it is one of the grand keys of the
navigation between the eastern and western states. It forms an
example of rapid progression astonishing, even in the States.
In 1814, the place was destroyed by the British, and only one
house left standing; in 1830, it contained 6,321 inhabitants, and
in 1·40, the population had increased to 18,356. The distance
to Albany, by stage, is 284 miles; and, by the Erie canal, 363
miles. Lines of railway have been commenced at Albany and
Buffalo, and are being laid down in the direction of the canal,
and will, doubtless, at no distant period, accompany it throughout its entire length.

An extract from a financial report of the state of New York, may serve to give some idea, not only of the importance of Buffalo, but also of the immense natural resources of the western states. After giving some statements relative to the influence of the Erie Canal on its immediate neighbourhood, and on the state of New York generally, the report proceeds to state the present extent of commerce with the west, and the probable future results to be derived from commercial intercourse with those regions.

" The western termination of the Erie Canal" (at Buffalo) " looks out upon Lake Erie, the most southerly and central of that great chain of navigable lakes, which stretches far into the interior from our western boundary, Around these inland seas a cluster of five great states is rapidly rising. The territory which they comprise, and which is to become tributary to the canal, embraces that great area, extending from the lakes on the north to the Ohio in the south, and from the western confines of this state to the upper Mississippi, containing 280,000 square miles. To measure its extent by well-known objects, it is fifteen times as large as that part of the state of New York, west of the county of Oneida—nearly twice as large as the kingdom of France—and about six times as extensive as the whole of England. It contains 180,000,000 of acres of arable land, a large portion of which is of surpassing fertility.

" In the brief period of twenty-one years, such has been the influx of population into this great district, that Ohio, the eldest member of this brotherhood of nations, now numbers 1,400,000 inhabitants, Indiana upwards of 600,000, Illinois and Michigan, (both of whom have organized governments, and came into the Union) 700,000 ; while, west of Lake Michigan, not only is Wisconsin rapidly rising, but even beyond the upper Mississippi, 30,000 citizens have already laid the foundations of yet another state. Such is the onward march of this population, that the amount of its annual increase alone exceeds in number the white inhabitants of ten of the states in the Union. The population already embraced within the district in question falls short of three millions, and if the same rate of progress shall be maintained for the twelve years next to come, by 1850 it will exceed six millions.

" This group of inland states has two outlets for its trade to the ocean ; one by the Mississippi to the Gulf of Mexico ; the other through Lake Erie and the navigable communications of this state to the Atlantic. Whether it be attributable to similarity of origin, or laws, or habits, or consanguinity, or superior salubrity of climate, their people evidently prefer the market in the Atlantic, and they are making prodigious efforts to reach it. Three great canals (one of them longer than the Erie Canal), embracing in their aggregate length one thousand miles, are to connect the Ohio with Lake Erie, while another deep and capacious channel, excavated for nearly thirty miles through solid rock, unites Lake Michigan with the navigable waters of the Illinois. In addition to these broad avenues of trade, they are also constructing lines of railroads, not less than 1,500 miles in extent, in order to reach, with more ease and speed, the lakes through which they seek a conveyance to a sea-board. The undaunted resolution of this energetic race of men is strikingly evinced by the fact, that the cost of the works which they have thus undertaken (and most of which are in actual progress), will exceed forty-eight millions of dollars, a sum far exceeding all that New York, with two millions of inhabitants, and two hundred years of accumulated wealth, has ever attempted. The circumstance, moreover, is particularly important, that the public works of each of these great communities are arranged on a harmonious plan, each having a main line supported and enriched by lateral and tributary branches, thereby bringing the industry of their whole people into prompt and profitable action, while the systems themselves are again united on a grander scale, in a series of systems, comprising an· aggregate length of more than 2,500 miles, with Lake Erie as its common centre.

" It is estimated that the agricultural products which annually descend the Mississippi and its tributaries have already reached 70,000,000 dollars. The value of the property transported on the canals of the state of New York, during the year 1836, is shown by official tables to be 67,000,000 dollars. Of that amount it may be estimated that 50,000,000 dollars consisted of property belonging exclusively to a portion of the population of this state, not exceeding a million and a half in number, being at the rate of 33 dollars 33 cents for each inhabitant; and the amount which they paid for its transportation exceeded two millions of dollars. If the same scale of production and consumption shall be assumed for the population in the district in question (and no reason is perceived why it should not be), the six millions of inhabitants in the West, who will resort to the Erie Canal for the means of conveyance, will furnish tonnage in exports, and imports, of at least 200,000,000 of dollars in value. The experience of other nations will shew that this amount is not over estimated. The food produced in England alone in the year 1835, by an agricultural population of about eight millions, was valued by their political economists at 604,000,000 dollars; and that of France was ascertained by its minister of finance to be 5,237,000,000 francs, or 980,000,000 dollars.

"But there are peculiar reasons why the proportion of agricultural exports of this great inland population should far exceed that of other nations. The exuberance of their soil, the salubrity of their climate, and the cheapness of their lands (arising from the vast supply within their limits), will enable them always to furnish food to every other portion of the continent, on more advantageous terms than it can be elsewhere produced. Labour there reaps its best reward, and harvests of an hundred fold repay its exertions ; and such will always be the superior productiveness of this region, that when the great series of public works shall be completed, and a bushel of wheat on the plains of Indiana shall be brought within a few cents in price of a bushel in New England, its production in New England must cease. The same cause will probably operate to change the culture of portions even of our own state; for the unequalled fertility of the West will always enable it to supply those products requiring richness of soil with a less amount of labour, and, consequently, at a cheaper rate, than they can be produced within our own borders.

" We know that the western part of our own state is increasing in numbers with considerable rapidity, and yet that it furnishes an export of at least 20,000,000 dollars in value. The states of the West, around the lakes, by the year 1845 will probably hold the same relative position in respect to the whole of the Erie Canal, which the counties of New York, west of the Seneca lake now bear to that part of the line east of Utica. Our trade will then be measured, not by counties, but by 'sovereign states, themselves containing their fifty counties ; and our revenues, no longer dependent on the villages and townships scattered along the borders of the canal, will be drawn from the wide spread and populous communities, inhabiting the broad expanse between the Ohio and the lakes."*

* This extract is taken from Buckingham's America.

A

CHAPTER VIII.

On landing, the shorter the stay the emigrant bound for the interior can make, the better, as it saves both time and money. During the voyage out, any person of ordinary tact can gain much information which may be of future benefit to him, particularly regarding his operations at the seaport to which he is bound.

As my remarks refer principally to the state of Illinois,* I shall bestow attention chiefly on the routes leading to the different parts of that portion of the Mississippi Valley; giving some of the intermediate places and distances.

Emigrants to the states generally land at New York. Should the destination of the emigrant be to any part of Illinois south of St. Louis, it will be most to his advantage to take a route leading to the Ohio river, as he can drop down it to the Wabash; which forms the boundary of the state on the east, for a distance of two hundred miles of boatable water; thence he can run along the southern extremity of the state to the point at the junction of the Ohio and Mississippi; and sailing up the Mississippi, which forms the western boundary, can take any of the intermediate landings between the point and St. Louis.

One route from New York to the Ohio, is by Philadelphia to Pittsburg.

ROUTE FROM NEW YORK, BY PHILADELPHIA, TO PITTSBURG.

			Miles.
To South Amboy, by steamboat	...	...	25
By railroad to Bordentown	...	...	33½– 58½
By steamboat to Philadelphia	...	...	29— 87½

The state of Illinois lies between 37 degrees and 42 degrees 30 minutes north latitude, and between 87 degrees 20 minutes and 91 degrees 20 minutes longitude west from Greenwich. It is about 380 miles long, and somewhat over 200 miles broad, at its widest part; containing an area, including the part of Lake Michigan within its boundaries, of 59,000 square miles; somewhat more than England and Wales, whose superficies is 57,960 square miles. The outline of the state, 1160 miles, is said, with the exception of 305 miles, to consist of navigable waters.

Miles.

By railroad to Harrisburg on the Susquehanna river 119—206

BY CANAL.

To Juniata river	...	...	...	...	15—221
Millerstown	...	...	...	...	17—238
Mifflin	...	...	...	...	17—255
Lewiston	...	...	...	...	13—268
Waynesburg	...	...	...	...	14—282
Hamiltonville	...	...	...	...	11—293
Huntingdon	...	...	...	...	7—300
Petersburg	...	...	...	...	8—308
Alexandria	...	...	...	...	23—331
Frankstown and Hollidaysburg		...	...		3—334

BY RAILROAD ACROSS THE MOUNTAINS

To Johnstown	...	...	...	...	38—372

BY CANAL

To Blairsville	...	...	...	...	35—407
Saltzburg	...	...	...	...	18—425
Warren	...	...	...	...	12—437
Alleghany river		...	...	...	16—453
Pittsburg	...	...	...	...	28—481

Passengers with freight or heavy luggage, ought to go from New York to Philadelphia by the "Transportation Line" of boats, via Delaware and Raritan Canal, and from Philadelphia, ought to take the same line of boats, or at least one bearing the same name, which professes to carry both passengers and luggage or freight through to Pittsburg in from 6½ to 8 days. Meals on the boats cost about 37½ cents.

The fare of the packets on this line, advertising to go through in five days, is seven dollars ; whilst the "Pioneer" and "Good Intent Lines" advertise to go through in four days, at ten dollars. Passengers pay for meals. All the lines are, for the most part, somewhat longer in performing the journey than the time specified in the advertisements.

STEAMBOAT ROUTE FROM PITTSBURG TO THE MOUTH OF THE OHIO.

Miles.

To Middletown, Pa.	...	...	...	...	10
Economy	...	...	...	...	8—18
Beaver	...	...	...	...	12—30
Georgetown	...	...	...	...	13—43
Wellsville, O.	...	...	...	...	7—50
Steubenville	...	...	...	...	20—70
Wellsburg, Va.	...	...	...	...	7—77

A 2

Miles.

To Warren, O.	...	...	...	6— 83
Wheeling, Va.	...	...	...	9— 92
Sistersville	...	...	...	40—132
Newport, O.	...	...	...	27—159
Marietta	...	...	...	15—174
Vienna, Va.	...	...	...	6—180
Parkersburg	...	...	...	5—185
Belpre and Blennerhassett's Island	...	...		2—187
Troy, O.	...	...	...	12—199
Belleville, Va.	...	...	...	5—204
Letarts Rapids	...	...	...	28—232
Point Pleasant	...	...	...	30—262
Gallipolis, O.	...	...	...	3—265
Guyandot, Va.	...	...	...	35—300
Burlington, O.	...	...	...	7—307
Greenupsburg, Ky.	...	...	...	23—330
Concord, O.	...	...	...	12—342
Portsmouth	...	...	...	8—350
Alexandria	...	...	...	2—352
Vanceburg, Ky.	...	...	...	18—370
Manchester, O.	...	...	...	16—386
Maysville, Ky., and Aberdeen, O.	...	...	11—397
Charleston, Ky.	...	...	...	7—404
Ripley, O.	...	...	...	5—409
Levana, O., and Dover, Ky.	...	...	3—412
Augusta, Ky.	...	...	...	2—414
Mechanicsburg, O.	...	...	...	7—421
Neville	...	...	...	3—424
Moscow	...	...	...	3—427
Point Pleasant	...	...	...	4—431
New Richmond	...	...	...	4—435
Columbia	...	...	...	13—448
Cincinnati, O., and Covington and Newport, Ky.			8—456
North Bend	...	...	...	17—473
Laurenceburg, Ia.	...	...	...	7—480
Aurora	...	...	...	3—483
Petersburg, Ky.	...	...	...	2—485
Belleview	...	...	...	7—492
Rising Sun, Ia.	...	...	...	3—495
Warsaw, Ky.	...	...	...	20—515
Vevay, Ia. and Ghent, Ky.	...	...	11—526
Port William, Ky.	...	...	...	8—534
Madison, Ia.	...	...	...	14—548

Miles.

To New London	...	...	...	...	7—555
Bethlehem	...	...	...	...	6—561
Westport, Ky.	...	...	...	...	6—567
Jeffersonville, Ia.		...	...	...	19—586
Louisville, Ky.	...	...	...	...	1—587
Shippingport	...	...	...	...	3—590
Portland, Ky. and New Albany, Ia.	...		...	...	1—591
West Point, Ky.		...	...	...	20—611
Brandenburg	...	...	...	...	18—629
Mauckport, Ia.	...	...	...	...	3—632
Leavenworth	...	...	...	...	14—646
Fredonia	...	...	...	...	2—648
Stephensport, Ky., and Rome, Ia.		...	...	...	34—682
Cloverport, Ky.		...	...	...	10—692
Troy, Ia.	...	...	...	...	21—713
Rockport	...	...	...	...	16—729
Owenboro, Ky.	...	...	...	...	12—741
Evansville, Ia.	...	...	...	...	36—777
Henderson, Ky.	...	...	...	...	12—789
Mount Vernon, Ia.		...	...	...	28—817
Carthage, Ky.	...	...	...	...	13—830
Wabash River	...	...	...	...	7—837
Raleigh, Ky.		...	...	...	6—843
Shawneetown, Ills.	...	...	...	...	6—849
Battery Rock ...		...	...	...	12—861
Cave in Rock ...		...	...	...	9—870
Tower Rock ...		...	...	...	5—875
Golconda, Ills.		...	...	...	15—890
Smithland, mouth of the Cumberland River					18—908
Paducah, mouth of the Tennessee River			...		12—920
Fort Massac, Ills.		...	...	...	8—928
Caledonia	...	...	...	...	23—951
America	...	...	...	...	3—954
Trinity	...	...	...	...	5—959
Junction of the Ohio and Mississippi Rivers					6—965

STEAMBOAT ROUTE FROM THE MOUTH OF THE OHIO TO
ST. LOUIS.

To Elk Island	...	...	...	8
Dog-tooth Island	...	...	...	8—16
English Island ...		...	...	15—31
Cape Girardeau, Mo.	...	...	...	12—43
Bainbridge	...	...	...	10—53
Lacouse's Island	...	...	...	31—84

A 3

				Miles.
Kaskaskia River, near Chester, Ills.		...		15— 99
River au Vases	...	...	...	10—109
St. Genevieve, Mo.	...	...	...	9—118
Fort Chartres Island	...	...	...	10—128
Rush Island	...	...	...	10—138
Herculaneum, Mo.	...	...	...	10—148
Harrison, Ills.	...	...	...	1—149
Merrimac River	...	...	...	11—160
Carondolet, Mo.	...	...	...	13—173
St. Louis	...	...	...	7—180

According to one of the guide books, " The whole expense of a single person from New York to St Louis, by way of Philadelphia and Pittsburg, with cabin passage on the river, will range between 40 dollars, and 45 dollars, time from twelve to fifteen days.—Taking the transportation lines on the Pennsylvania Canal, and a deck passage on the steamboat, the expenses will range between 20 dollars, and 25 dollars, supposing the person buys his meals at 25 cents, and eats twice a day. If he carry his own provisions, the passage, &c., will be from 15 dollars to 18 dollars."

This nearly coincides with my own experience ; but, at the same time, it would be safe to calculate on the fares being somewhat higher, as they vary considerably, according to circumstances ; say, for cabin passage from New York to St Louis, meals included.

				döl. c.	dol. c.
To Philadelphia	...	...	...	3 50 to	3 50
Pittsburg...	...	...	...	12	16
Cincinnati	...	...	...	10	15
Louisville	...	...	...	4	6
St. Louis...	...	...	...	12	18
				41 50	58 50

A deck passage, without meals, may be stated as follows :—

To Philadelphia	...	...	...	1 to	1
Pittsburg...	...	...	...	4	6
Cincinnati	...	...	...	3	5
Louisville	...	...	...	1	2
St. Louis	...	...	...	4	6
				13	20

The place for deck passengers is the deck on which are the engine and boilers ; it is enclosed on the sides, and is situated immediately below the cabin deck ; the cabin again being surmounted by a third deck, termed the hurricane deck, which covers in the whole.

The cabin fares on the western rivers always include meals. The deck passenger must carry bedding and food, or take his meals with the crew of the boat, at 25 cents a meal.

Should the emigrant be desirous of going to the northern part of Illinois, the best route will be from New York, by Buffalo, to Chicago, on the southern extremity of Lake Michigan; and this is the best route, not only for the north of St. Louis, but for a large proportion of the state, in autumn, when the Ohio is apt to become too low for the passage of steamboats.

STEAMBOAT AND CANAL ROUTE FROM NEW YORK TO CHICAGO, ILLINOIS.

				Miles.	
To Albany, by steamboat ...	...	...	...	145	
Buffalo, by Erie Canal ...	...	...	...	363—	508

ROUTE FROM BUFFALO TO CHICAGO BY LAKE STEAMER.

To Dunkirk, N.Y.	...	...	...	39—	547
Portland ...	...	...	...	18—	565
Erie, Pa. ...	...	...	...	35—	600
Ashtabula, O.	...	...	...	39—	639
Fairport ...	...	...	...	32—	671
Cleveland, O.	...	...	...	30—	701
Sandusky ...	...	...	...	54—	755
Amherstburg, U.C.	...	...	...	52—	807
Detroit, Mich.	...	...	...	18—	825
Point au Barques	...	...	...	160—	985
Mackinaw ...	...	...	,...	195—1180	
Big Beaver Island	...	...	...	55—1235	
Manitou Isles	...	...	...	40—1275	
Milwauky, Wis. Ter.	...	...	...	180—1455	
Chicàgo, Ills.	...	...	...	81—1536	

The expences, by this route, are nearly as under:—

				dol.	dol.
From New York to Albany by barge attached to steamer ...	...	...	...	1 to	1
Albany to Buffalo	...	...	...	3	5
Buffalo to Chicàgo	...	...	...	12	15
				16	21

The above is for deck passage, and does not include meals.

A passage from Buffalo to Chicàgo may be had, in one of the lake schooners, for less than half the fare charged by the steamers; but those vessels are sometimes several weeks on the voyage, whilst the steamers accomplish it in five or six days.

The fare on the Erie Canal, for those who provide their own food and bedding, is about 1½ cents; and for those who board with the captain 2½ cents per mile. Should the passenger be desirous of providing his own food whilst on the canal, he can do so with little difficulty, as there are numerous towns and villages along the line, and he is allowed the cooking apparatus of the boat; but not till the captain's passengers and crew have done with them.

Those who can afford it, and are not encumbered with luggage have the choice of railroad for a considerable part of the line, and for the rest the packet boats, exclusively for passengers, on which the fare is four cents a mile, board included, and which go at the rate of five miles an hour; whilst those carrying both freight and passengers may accomplish about half that speed.

Between Chicàgo and St. Louis there is not yet water conveyance through, but a canal is being made, which, it is said, will be finished in 1844 at farthest, and which will connect Lake Michigan with the boatable waters of the Illinois river at Peru, a distance of between ninety and one hundred miles from Chicàgo. A waggon can be had from Chicàgo to Peru for about fifteen dollars, which will convey a family of three or four, and a considerable amount of luggage. Stage fare is about six cents a mile. Meals, at the stage houses, thirty-seven and a half cents.

ROUTE FROM PERU TO ST. LOUIS BY STEAMER.

					Miles.
To Peoria	...	...	...	...	58
Pekin	...	...	...	...	6— 64
Havannah	...	...	...	...	33— 97
Beardstown	...	...	...	...	38—135
Meredosia	...	...	...	...	16—151
Naples	...	...	...	...	6—157
Motezuma	...	...	...	...	20—177
Grafton	...	...	...	...	58—235
St. Louis, Mo.	...	...	...	...	37—272

I am not acquainted with the fares on this route; but, comparing them with those of other routes on the western rivers, should think four dollars a sufficiently high estimate.

There is still another route from New York to the southern parts of Illinois, branching off from the preceding one at Cleveland, and by the Ohio and Erie Canal, leading to the Ohio river, at Portsmouth; where it joins the route from New York by Philadelphia and Pittsburg. It is about 170 miles longer than the route last mentioned; the additional distance will add two or three dollars to the expences.

Perhaps the best route from Britain to any part of the Mississippi Valley, and decidedly the best to those parts adjacent to the Mississippi or Missouri rivers, is by New Orleans. The only disadvantage attending this route is, that vessels direct from British ports cannot be had at all times; but the difference in expence, between this and the eastern routes, is so material, that a little time and money would be well bestowed in obtaining it. I am aware of an instance of an emigrant going from Liverpool to Peoria, 180 miles above St. Louis, for five pounds sterling, and in all cases the difference in expence would be nearly one-half. There is no difficulty or delay at New Orleans, as steamers are daily leaving for St. Louis and Cincinnati. The cabin fare from New Orleans to Cincinnati, a distance of 1547 miles, is about 25 dollars; and it is reasonable to suppose that the fare to St. Louis, a distance of 1218, will not be more. The deck fare is seldom more, and is frequently less than one third of that of the cabin; at which rate the deck passage from New Orleans to St. Louis would be about 8 dollars.

In all cases a bargain ought to be made for the freight or extra luggage, at so much per 100 lbs.; with a clear understanding how much the passenger shall be allowed to carry free of charge; and this is particularly necessary on the western waters, where the fares are, in a great measure, regulated by the number of boats about to start. In a general way 50 lbs. on the canal boats, and 100 lbs. on the steamers, are allowed, free of charge, for each adult. The price of freight on the canals is about twenty-five cents per 100 lbs. for one hundred miles. By the steamers it is somewhat lower. The fare for children below 12 years of age is one-half of that for adults.

The less luggage the emigrant has, beyond what is absolutely necessary, the better; but should there be a considerable quantity, it ought to be divided into packages that can be easily managed by two people. Each package ought to have the owner's name, or initials, with a number legibly painted upon it; as it is much easier, in the sometimes hurried transference from one conveyance to another, to see that the number is complete, than to tax the memory by individualizing each; besides it may be of use to make a list of the articles contained in each number, so that in case anything should be wanted on the journey, it may be known, by referring to the list, in which number the article is contained. It is a waste of money to take out furniture of almost any kind, as it is very liable to be smashed to pieces, and, when it does arrive safe at its destination, is frequently found to be altogether inappropriate. He is a poor mechanic, who cannot make most of the furnishings of a shanty, and a shanty, or camping out, is likely to be the fate of an emigrant and his family for some time at least, unless he have friends who will shelter him. He may lodge in a boarding-house in some town, but that is expensive ; besides he has no need of his furniture there, which will be incurring a constantly accumulating expense in storage and other dues.

As soon as the emigrant arrives at his destination, which ought not to be far from some navigable river, or other outlet for produce, his first care, if he intend to purchase land, will be to fix upon a proper location ; and this, to a stranger, is a matter of no small difficulty. If he have friends in the country, or have letters of introduction from some mutual friend to any who have previously emigrated, this difficulty is easily got over, otherwise it will be better to trust to the advice even of strangers than to his own judgement, as any previous experience he may have had will not be sufficient to direct him in a country where so much must be new to him. Of course he will not place implicit confidence in the advice of any who may have interested motives.

As a healthy situation is of the greatest importance, care ought to be taken in securing one ; and in this particular, the emigrant will find himself as much at a loss, as in any on which he has to exercise his judgment, for no matter what the situation, or the part of the country be, the reply to a question regarding its healthiness will almost invariably be favourable.— " Is your settlement a healthy one, sir ?"—" Oh, yes, quite healthy."—" What do you think of the country on the other side of the river ?"   " Well, guess its full of ague ; and the way in which the mosquitos fix one is a caution ; 'taint fit for nothing but a bullfrog or a half-breed Frenchman."—" But you have ague here sometimes, have not you ?"—" Oh yes, but 'taint of no account."   Go over to the other side of the river and the answers will most likely be to the same effect.

The undulating prairies, exposed to every breeze, are beyond doubt the most healthy, and although they are swept at intervals, during the short winters which prevail, by the piercing north-west wind chilled by a temperature at zero, yet ample amends is made by the refreshing day breeze which regularly fans them during the heats of summer ; making them tolerable when the woods and bottoms are hot almost to suffocation ; besides a few years, with very little expense and trouble, will raise a barrier of trees to oppose the wind from the cold points ; and last, though not least, there are few or no mosquitos on the rolling prairies; a boon which can be properly estimated only by those who have experienced the annoyance of those pests.

Next to the prairies, the summit or immediate back of the bluffs on the Mississippi, is said to be most healthy, as there is generally a breeze blowing up or down the river. There may be something too, in the bluffs being higher, particularly when rocky, than the general face of the country; the land sloping back for some distance into the interior; and the springs and rivulets running, often at right angles, and in some instances, for miles directly contrary to the course of the river, till they join some creek which has forced a passage through the bluff, or has found no bluff to contend with farther down the country.

A few feet above the general level may appear of small consequence, yet such is not the case; and those situations are universally esteemed healthy. They may be islands in the sea of miasm; an illustration perhaps not altogether fanciful, as very little observation is necessary to convince any one with ordinary senses, that the bottoms and valleys branching out from them, are frequently filled with an atmosphere of very different quality from that on the ridges and higher grounds; particularly towards sunset and through the night. This atmosphere has a foetid smell; is comparatively cold, uncomfortably so to a person who is thinly clad; and in calm weather, level on the surface, for a person may wade into it up to the neck, and then duck his head in and out.

The bottoms, or alluvial flats on the rivers, are all more or less unhealthy; but it is said that if a settlement is made there, the nearer it is to the bank of the river the better. It is a feature of the western rivers, that the bottoms* are frequently more elevated near the river than farther back towards the bluffs*, where they are often marshy and abounding in stagnant lagoons and backwaters, which are filled, when the river overflows its banks at the periodical risings or freshets, and on the subsidence of the waters, are left full of vegetable matter to putrify in an almost tropical sun. These are the chosen abodes of myriads of piping toads and frogs, water snakes, mud turtles, and several kinds of fish, of such qualities and appearance as one might naturally expect to meet with in such villainous places. The want of wholesome water is a serious objection to settling on bottom lands; water no doubt can be had by sinking

* By "bottom" is meant the level ground at the sides of rivers, creeks, &c. Every Scotchman will understand me, when I tell him it is synonymous with the word "haugh" or "holm." The bluffs are the rising ground or at the lateral termination of the bottoms. They are sometimes precipitous like our scaurs, and at others form fine banks sweeping down to the plain.

to no great depth in any part of them, but it is universally impregnated with something imparting to it deleterious qualities and a nauseous taste, and frequently looks as if hay had been steeped in it. Indeed the water in the branches and creeks, muddy though it be, is esteemed more wholesome than that of these wells. Add to this, the equal to Egyptian plague of mosquitos, a plague seldom ending day or night for many months in the year, and there is a fitting climax to all the other evils.

On rivers, and marshes, the western is esteemed healthier than the eastern side; as the prevailing winds during the summer and autumn months are from the west, or some of the neighbouring points.

If the emigrant be single, it will be his wisest course not to be hasty in the selection of a farm, for if a mechanic* in any of the ordinary trades, he can easily procure work in some of the towns in the prairies, till such time as he may become acquainted with the country and the habits of the people. If he have previously been a farmer, or farm servant, he can board himself with some farmer on the prairie, for a dollar a-week; and will be very unlucky, indeed, if he cannot make instead of losing money, if he should only work half the time; seeing a labouring man can obtain a dollar a day and his board.

When the emigrant has a family, his best course will be to make a settlement as speedily as possible, and he need not be very many days, after having pitched upon a spot, in raising a few huts or shanties; for he has nothing to do but to go round among his neighbours, and request their assistance, which will be cheerfully rendered without any remuneration, except good cheer, and, it may be, future assistance of a similar kind. A more comfortable dwelling, and other accommodation, can be supplied by the same means, when the more pressing concerns are disposed of; but before this takes place, it ought to be ascertained if water can be had near to the spot fixed upon. This can be done either by boring, or what is perhaps quite as cheap a method, by sinking a well at once; an affair of no great difficulty, as the prairie is almost one entire bed of alluvial matter. Water is generally got at a depth of about thirty feet, and, what is singular, the higher the situation, the greater is the certainty of finding water at a moderate depth. I do not pretend to account for this, but it is a circumstance, the truth of which, though often asserted, I never heard doubted, and which

---

* I am here supposing the emigrant to be desirous of buying land, for it would be needless for a mechanic to go so far west as Illonois, as, if a good workman, he could easily procure employment farther east.

my own experience inclines me to credit.* I have noticed, however, that the alluvion on the most elevated parts of the prairie, is often not so deep as in the lower situations ; as rock of some kind is frequently found in sinking wells, and thus there may be struck springs, or the water discharged from springs and collected from other sources, which will naturally circulate between the alluvion and the denser materials below. That there are springs, any one may be satisfied by examining the bluffs on the river courses, where they are frequently in great abundance.

Should the emigrant be desirous of having a frame or brick house he must employ regular mechanics

I ought to mention, that it is only at the *raising* of the house that the stranger will receive assistance a second time. He must, either himself or with hired assistance, cut down the timber, log it off at the proper lengths, and score or hew it down on two opposite sides to the proper thickness (about nine inches) ; he must also cut timber, and split it for clapboards and shingles, for roofing and weather-boarding ; then he must prepare joists and spars, which are laid lengthwise between the gables instead of couples ; and lastly, must have all hauled to the spot. At this stage the assistance of his neighbours is requested, who, on their arrival, proceed to portion themselves off into gangs with a determinate job for each. As the notching, or dove-tailing the corners, is an operation requiring considerable adroitness, those who are considered to be the best handlers of the axe, or to have most experience in that part of the work are selected as corner-men ; each standing on a corner and there notching, fitting and squaring off his end of the log, as it is raised up to him, with great dexterity and precision. After three or four rounds are on the walls, sloping spars are applied to them, and the logs are rolled up, at first with the hands, and finally with forked sticks. This operation, when the logs are green and heavy, requires a good deal of hands ; as there ought to be at least two gangs, each capable of hoisting up a log, and each taking charge of a side and an end of the building, so that the logs at the opposite sides or ends may be raised simultaneously. The logs are not laid quite close, an interval of two or three inches being left between each, which is afterwards *chunk-d* and *daubed* i. e. filled up with bits of wood, and plastered with clay or mortar ; the two hewn sides thus forming the outer and inner surfaces of the wall.

In the cities and more populous parts, the clapboards are

* The rolling prairies are here referred to, and not bottoms, marshes, or basins, the receptacles of all the water circulating through the soil of a tract of country.

B

made, perhaps about twenty inches in length, of pine, or some other wood that splits freely, and does not warp, and are nailed on like slates; but in the newer districts, they are about four feet long, and, though sometimes nailed on, are frequently held down by heavy transverse spars, kept at the proper distances by blocks of wood. In this manner the walls of a substantial log-house are raised, and the roof put on, often in one day, without so much as a nail being used.

Next comes the sawing out of the apertures for doors and windows, and space at one end for a fireplace. In the log-houses of the West there are, in such a house as I have described, generally two doors, one in each side, in order to secure the luxury of a current of air through the house in hot weather, and very often to light the interior; for it is sometimes a difficult matter to get window frames. When the season becomes cold, the door exposed to the wind is shut; and in the short periods of extreme cold, when both are shut, the room is sufficiently cheerful from the effects of a roaring fire. In the gable is cut the opening for the fireplace, which, with the chimney, is outside, and is sometimes built of brick or stone, but much more frequently of wood plastered over with mud.

Sleepers being laid down, and plank procured, if there is a saw-mill in the neighbourhood, the floor is laid down, often without being nailed or jointed. In lack of plank, trees are split up into what are termed puncheons, of three or four inches in thickness, which are laid down on the sleepers, and, with a little care in hewing and fitting, make a very good floor.

There is frequently met with a habitation consisting of two apartments such as the one I have described, built in the same line, with their gables ten or twelve feet apart; the intervening space and all under one roof. This space, which is called a stoop, or porch, is floored, and, in summer, is the resort of the inmates when at meals or enjoying the shade. Sometimes the roof is made to project, so that there is, in front of the house, a stoop of five or six feet wide supported on posts; but this is not so sure to catch a breeze as the other.

As soon as possible, other buildings, such as a smoke-house, stable, corn-cribs, barn, &c., are added. The smoke-house is generally used as a larder or store-house for provisions, milk, &c., except at the season when the pork is cured and smoked: the latter operation being universally practiced.

Fencing the farm is an operation requiring speedy attention, as without it no crop is secure from the depredations of cattle and horses, which roam over the prairies and through the woods at will; all land which is not enclosed being common. The almost universal fence is the zig zag or worm fence, which is constructed of split rails. A tree being selected by the chopper is cut down, logged off into lengths of ten feet, and split with wedges and the axe. In the bottoms where the timber is good, many trees will make four or five cuts without a limb; affording from 150 to 200 heavy rails. It is reckoned a good day's work for a man to cut down, log off, and split up such a tree into rails. From 100 to 150 rails among timber, is a good day's work; among timber of inferior quality of course so many cannot be made.

At first sight the worm fence appears very inefficient, but on a closer inspection and more intimate acquaintance with its qualities it improves in ones estimation, and it would certainly be difficult for the pioneer settler to substitute anything so efficient and at the same time so easily to be got. Stone is not to be had on the prairies, except on the banks of rivers and creeks, where it sometimes appears in the bluffs; but if it even were at hand, it would be to quarry and haul, and would cost more labour and money than cutting and hauling rails; and then every man is not a mason, but any man of ordinary physical powers can put up 200 yards of a rail fence in a day, or fence about 30 acres in a week; and, when the timber is good, such a fence, with some repairs, will last ten or twelve years. The fences generally consist of eight or nine rails, and, if the rails be strong, may be in the one instance, about 4½ or 5 feet, and in the other about 6 feet high when made with stake and rider, which is done by sinking on opposite sides of the fence, at each corner where the ends of the rails are piled upon one another, two stakes of about 8 feet long, and causing their upper ends to cross over the fence. Into this cross or angle is laid one end of the rider, the other end being laid into the similar angle at the next corner; thus at once heightening the fence and binding it at each corner. This is the legal fence, which, if broken through by cattle, entitles the owner to damages, which cannot be claimed when the fence is without stake and rider.

Seeing it is absolutely necessary that the cultivated land should be fenced, the settler must endeavour to procure a farm, with a sufficient quantity of timber upon it, for that purpose. This he may chance to find a matter of considerable difficulty where there are many settlements, as the first settlers have not only pitched upon the spots most favoured in that respect, but have without exception, and in defiance of the law, ransacked all the government lands within reach; never cutting a stick of their own for any purpose so long as there is any suitable that can be stolen from U. S. or Uncle Sam as they facetiously term the United States government. But of all the destructives " your — tanner" is the worst. He with his myrmidons sallies forth axe in hand and levels in the dust the monarchs of the wood who haply have withstood the blasts of three hundred winters, and, having stripped them of their bark, leaves them to rot. To an Englishman who has an habitual reverence for fine timber, such destruction would appear, to say the least of it, very injudicious; but throughout the Union the inhabitants seem to be excited by a spirit if extermination against trees.

There can be no doubt that some other method of fencing will be resorted to at no distant period; and I do not think there will be any difficulty in making quick fences, as there are plenty of indigenous trees and shrubs, such as the wild apple, the plum, locust, &c., which thrive very well on almost any part of the prairie. The apple and plum can be raised in any quantity from the seed and stones; and I have seen the black locust which had been raised from seed, and, at the end of three years, had attained a height of upwards of twenty feet. There may often be noticed along a line of fence which has stood for a few years, such a growth of young trees, wild apples, and plums, as would make an inpregnable fence, with the addition of a few grape vines, and a little care bestowed in trimming. Grape vines abound in all the woods and run to a great length. They may frequently be seen attached to the limbs of trees at a height of seventy or eighty feet. But quick fences and many other improvements must be the result of time as the settler, for some years at least, is sufficiently occupied in obtaining the readiest and most necessary conveniences Where a man is possessed of that best source of riches in a new country, a family of stout sons, the means of comfort are soon attained; but where he has everything to attend to himself, it is quite impossible either that all should be done well, or that many necessary operations should not be altogether omitted.

Among the first cares of every one settling on a new place ought to be the planting out an orchard of apple trees;—the source of a simple and palatable luxury throughout the year— the apples being preserved by slicing them down and drying them in the sun. Some care ought to be taken in the selection of the trees, for when they are raised from the seed, as they almost invariably are in the back settlements, it sometimes happens, that out of one hundred trees there is not one bearing palatable fruit. This could easily be remedied, by going through among the neighbouring orchards and selecting cuttings from such as are known to be the best trees, and engrafting them either on stocks raised from seed or on the wild apple; which answers very well and is to be found all over the country.*

Nobody, after the first three or four years, need want peaches, as, by planting the stones in the corners of the zig zag fences, he will soon have trees; which grow with surprising rapidity; and a plentiful supply of fruit which, though not so large as the carefully selected kinds in Europe, yet is very delicious; and, being split and dried in the sun, forms a considerable addition to the somewhat meagre comforts of a new settler's table.

The apple and peach are sometimes so abundant that they are given to the hogs. The peaches however, are mostly preserved, and either hauled to market if there is one near, or taken to a distillery for the purpose of making peach brandy.

COST OF ERECTING A HOUSE 18 BY 20 FEET, AND OTHER BUILDINGS, &c.

	d.	c.
Six days cutting down and logging off trees, at 1 dollar per day	6	00
Six days hauling logs one mile, one man and two yoke of oxen, at 1 dollar 50 cents per day	9	00
Fourteen days hewing logs, at 1 dollar 50 cents per day	21	00
Cutting and hauling rafters	2	50
One thousand boards for roofing, at 1 dollar per 100	10	00
Nails for roofing	1	50
Putting on roof	5	00
200 boards for weather-boarding gable ends	2	00
Studding for nailing weather boards to	1	00
Sawing out two doors, one window, and a fireplace	1	00
720 feet of plank for flooring and lofting, at 2 dollars per 100	14	40
Laying down floors say eight days taken, the workman found in bed and board	12	00
Making and fitting-in doors	10	00
Making and fitting-in window	2	75
2000 bricks for chimney, at 5 dollars per 1000	10	00
5 bushels of lime, at 12½ cents per bushel	0	62½
	108	77½

* The inhabitants assert that tame cuttings will not grow on the wild stocks, but I proved this to be wrong by engrafting some which grew very well.

Carried forward   108 77½

3 days hauling of brick with two yoke of steers, at 2 dollars per day*	6 00	
Building chimney 5 dollars, and man to attend on bricklayer 2 dollars	7 00	
16 bushels of lime, at 12½ cents, for daubing the spaces between the logs	2 00	
Two days hauling lime and sand at 2 dollars per day	4 00	
Chunking, i. e., partially filling up the spaces between the logs with bits of wood	1 00	
Daubing, one hand four days, at 1 dollar per day ...	4 00	
Building (including all work) stable for two horses	15 00	
Building (including all work) a corn crib that will contain 500 bushels of unshocked corn ...	20 00	
Building smoke house	15 00	
Cow pen	7 00	
Digging well 30 feet deep, at 25 cents the perpendicular foot†	7 50	
Hauling stones, 15 loads, at an average of distances, one load per day, with two yoke of oxen at 2 dollars per day	30 00	
Building sides of well at 25 cents the perpendicular foot	7 50	
Furnishing well with roller, rope, and bucket, say ...	5 00	
Horse	100 00	
Cow	15 00	
Hogs and poultry	5 00	
Furniture	20 00	
Household expences, say for a family of four ...	50 00	
Saddle and bridle	10 00	

439 77½

COST OF BUYING, FENCING, AND IMPROVING 80 ACRES OF LAND
IN RANDOLPH COUNTY, ILLINOIS.

Purchasing 80 acres of land at 1 dollar 25 cents per acre	100 00	
Making 10,000 rails at 1 dollar per 100	100 00	

200 00

* It is here assumed that only one load of bricks can be hauled per day which, taking the average distances from where bricks are made, will be a tolerably correct estimate for Randolph County.

† The wells are always made as narrow as they can conveniently be worked.

	Carried forward	200 00

Hauling do. 3 miles	80	00
Building do. at 1 dollar per day	12	00
* To put 80 acres into fields of 20 acres requiring half the quantity of ring fence	96	00
Breaking up 80 acres at 2 dollars 50 cents per acre	200	00
† Planting sod corn requiring about one bushel to 4 acres at 30 cents per bushel	6	00
Sowing with wheat in the fall, one bushel of wheat per acre, at 80 cents per bushel	64	00
Sower, six days, at 1 dollar per day	6	00
Harrowing 12 days, at 1 dollar 50 cents per day ...	18	00
Cutting, hauling home, and setting up corn, at 1 dollar 50 cents per acre	120	00
Harvesting wheat, at 1 dollar 25 cents per acre ...	100	00
Hauling and stacking do. at 57 cents an acre ...	45	60
Thrashing by small thrashing mill hauled about the country; and which thrashes 100 bushels a day, at 6¼ cents a bushel; allowing the ground to have produced 22 bushels an acre§	110	00
Hauling to market a day's journey, or from 25 to 30 miles, at 12½ cents per bushel	220	00
	1277	60

VALUE OF PRODUCE RAISED FROM 80 ACRES OF LAND DURING TWO SEASONS WITH ONE PLOUGHING AND A HARROWING.

	d.	c.
80 acres of sod corn, 30 bushels per acre at 30 cents per bushel	720	00
80 acres of wheat producing 22 bushels per acre at 80 cents per bushel	1408	00

	d.	c.		
			2128	00
Deduct outlay for buildings, &c. ...	439	77½		
Do. for land, fencing, &c. ...	1277	60		
			1717	37½
			410	62½

* By a law of this state march fences are made and upheld at the mutual expense of the respective proprietors, if both derive benefit from such fences.
† The prairie plough goes without being held, and the ploughman scatters along every third or fourth furrow the seed which is covered in by the next round of the plough.
§ Treading out with horses will cost upwards of one half more than

From the preceding statements it will be seen that the farmer after having contracted for everything realizes a clear profit of 410 dollars 62½ cents from the land. And had he himself laboured would have encreased that sum to a very considerable amount.

It may be said, perhaps, that the wheat is valued too high, but the price assumed is nearly 30 cents less than the price of wheat during a plentiful season that I was in Randolph County, Illinois. Last year (1841), owing to the monetary convulsion in the United States the price had fallen, but the average price still was 80 cents a bushel and prices were looking up. Times were considered to have been very dull and prices low. But even admitting that there was no profit during the first two seasons the price of the land, fencing, buildings, &c. amounting (with the deduction of 50 dollars for household expences) to 777 dollars 77½ cents would afterwards be saved.

Were the farmer himself to labour he would require in addition to the things already mentioned,

	d.	c.
A pair of trained oxen　...　...　...	55	0
Waggon, plough, and gear for oxen ...　...	100	0
Axe　...　...　...　...　...	1	75
Wedges ...　...　...　...　...	1	0

	157	75

The case supposed above is an extreme one, and most likely wili never be reduced to practice. At the same time it may afford data for a greater variety of cases than if it had been confined within the bounds of actual practice in any individual instance ; and, in order the better to supply this desideratum, details of the different items have been given at some length.

Comparative view of the prices of produce in Randolph County, Ills., in the years 1830, 1837, and 1841.

	1830	1837	1841
	d. c.	d. c.	d. c.
Wheat, per bushel　...　...	0 50	1 25	0 80
Indian corn, per do.　...　...	0 21	0 50	0 36¼
Oats, per do.　...　...	0 35	0 35	0 36¼
Castor oil beans, per do.　...	0 75	1 13	1 25
Good horses, each　...　...	55 0	120 0	120 0

thrashing with the mill. A man and boy with four horses will tread out 25 bushels at an expense of 2 dollars 50 cents per day. For thrashing with the flail the eighth part is allowed ; the thrasher helping to clean the grain.

			1830		1837		1841	
			d.	c.	d.	c.	d.	d.
Cows, per head	...	...	8	0	17	0	15	0
Work Oxen a pair	...	...	45	0	70	0	55	0
Three years old steers		...	11	0	18	0	18	0
Three years old heifers		...	10	0	15	0	16	0
Beef, per 100 lbs.	...	...	2	0	3	75	4	50
Pork, per do.	...	...	2	0	3	75	3	0
* Mutton per ℔	...	...					0	6¼

CONCLUDING REMARKS.

Emigrants sometimes find difficulty, particularly when going to the west, in effecting a satisfactory exchange of money. Where gold is taken, of course, an exchange can always be effected in New York, or in the British Provinces, at the current rates; but when going to the far west, or indeed to any place far inland in the states, sovereigns must be disposed of at New York, or such seaport as the emigrant may land at. Should the sum be considerable, I think the emigrant will find it most to his interest to negotiate it by means of bills of exchange, for which he will receive a higher premium than for gold, as the risk of loss, and expence of negotiation are not so great. Good bills on London are marketable articles in all maritime cities in the world, and are frequently worth more than gold. As a still farther security against loss, the holder of the bills should at least have duplicates, or what is termed first and second of exchange, which enhances their value in a foreign market. In the case of bills, it will be necessary to have an introduction to some merchant, or other person of respectability, who is known to the money changers, and who will guarantee that you are the true holder.

Owing to the instability of the monetary affairs of the United States, it is almost impossible to give any advice about money, that shall be of service for many months. Should there be a substantial bank in New York or Philadelphia, it would, perhaps, be most advisable to deposit such money as the emigrant should not need on his journey west, and, for the amount, receive checques, which will increase in value as they are taken west. Such checques, and bills, at St. Louis, in 1837, obtained a premium ranging from two to seven per cent. Western money may be had at New York, with the recognised rate of exchange

* I do not know the price of sheep at present in Randolph County, but taking 48 lbs. as the average weight, and that will not be far from the mark, the carcase, at 6¼ cents per pound, would cost 3 dollars. I saw in 1838 a number of sheep of different ages sold for between 3 dollars and 4 dollars a-head.

between it and the eastern money, and, if the sum is not large
this method of disposing of it may be as good as any, as it saves
the trouble and expence of performing perhaps a long journey,
to some western city; but where the sum is large it is not so
safe. Bank notes, or Bills, as they are called, ought to be for
considerable sums, say 50 dollars or 100 dollars each; a number
of small bills being bulky and troublesome, and not so negotiatable
as the large ones in the west. The checques and bills are sold
in the west to merchants, who make yearly or half yearly journeys
to the east for goods. When the sum deposited in the bank is
large it is sometimes convenient to divide it into several sums,
having a checque for each, as, in that case, one can dispose of
either the whole, or a part, as may be found most advantageous.
In travelling west, it will be necessary to get rid of the money
of one state before entering another, otherwise the bills will not
pass, and in order to negotiate them with the banks or merchants, a discount will have to be submitted to; there will seldom
be any difficulty found in exchanging them at hotels on the borders of the different states.

Although no British coins pass current in the United States,
yet some of those of France, Spain, and Mexico do so. The
Spanish and Mexican dollars are considered equivalent to that of
the United States, but the French five franc piece, is generally
rated about 96, cents, or four cents less than a dollar.

The United States possess what is termed a 'decimal coinage,'
of which the dollar is the standard or primary unit. By this system the process of calculation is very much simplified and to
render cents (that is hundredths) into dollars, it is only necessary to point off the decimals; thus 1,00 cents are 1 dollar; or
10,35½ cents are in the same way understood as 10 dollars 35½
cents, and so on to any amount.

The metallic currency of the United States consists of the
double eagle of 10 dollars, eagle of 5 dollars, half eagle of 2 dollars and 50 cents, in gold; the dollar, half dollar, quarter dollar,
12½ cents, or York shilling, 10 cents or dime, 6¼ cents or York
sixpence 5 cents or half dime in silver, and the cent in copper.

The season in which I visited the United States was one
remarkable for sickness, and the southern and western states
suffered much, but with the exception of such visitations, it
would appear that the inhabitants of Illinois enjoy a very fair
amount of good health; indeed, it appeared to me, that they
were exempted from such a variety of diseases as we see in this
country —that there was some predisposing cause to bilious com-
plaints, to the exclusion of those of other types. There, as in

other parts of the world, much of the disease encountered is the result of rashness and folly; and no man of intemperate habits need expect to avoid the effects of such habits, merely by a change of country, more especially if the change be to a warmer climate.

Some people appear to think, that, if they were once across the Atlantic, they would have nothing else to do but to enjoy themselves; but they will find themselves mistaken. All must labour there, as well as in this country; the difference is, that, in America there is plenty of room and abundant remuneration for labour; whilst in Britain, the working population exceeds the demand, and, consequently, the price of labour is small: there is plenty to do, with plenty to live on, in the one county; and there is too little to do, and far too little for it in the other.

Where there is such a wide and varied field to choose from, many are apt to waver, and roam about from place to place in search of an El Dorado, which is never destined to bless their eyes. There is something enticing in the dreamy visions one gets, (like peeps into the realms of hope) of newer and fairer lands, whose praises come, borne along by the western winds, and which, like them, have no abiding place. I have met with men who had travelled thousands of miles, much of it on foot, and who seemed just as far from attaining their object as when they started. At one time the Valley of the Wabash was the rage; then it turned out that some part of Illinois, for instance Sangammon, was the right place; it was not long till some part of Missouri was the grand desideratum; that again was abandoned for Rock River, which, in turn, gave place to Ouisconsin, and now, I believe, some weary with wandering about the states, have left them, and clearing the Rocky Mountains at a bound, have landed in California.

Although I visited some parts of Canada, the number of works about that country, already before the public, render any fresh remarks supererogatory. My only reason for alluding to the country at all, is merely to state, as my decided opinion, that it does not, at present, afford such facilities for emigrants, as are to be met with in many parts of the United States. Canada, however, possesses one advantage over the western states in the greater salubrity of its climate; a circumstance which may be allowed to counter-balance many disadvantages. The climate of the eastern and middle states, differs little, as regards healthiness, from that of Canada.

At present, a feeling of mistrust has been engendered by the

ominous accounts which have emanated from the other side of
the Atlantic, and by the return to Britain of numbers who had
emigrated. Now, nothing is more certain than that there has
been great derangement in money matters—that there has been
a want of employment for labour, and consequently, that there
has been some privation. But, whilst this is true, it is not the
less certain that distress has not afflicted all parts of the country
to the same extent—that the western settler has not felt the
pressure of the times, nor been so much forced to increase his
exertions for subsistence, as has the inhabitant of the thickly
peopled, and more artificial Eastern states.

Civilization induces artifical wants, which must be artificially
supplied, and, when any impediment occurs to the onward course
of affairs, in civilized communities, want must be the result to a
large proportion of the people, who have nothing to rely on for
subsistence, beyond the immediate fruits of their daily labour.
In such communities, are to be found the greatest amount of
wealth, and the greatest amount of poverty. The wealthy are
enabled to contend with the difficulty to an extent in some measure proportioned to their means : at all events to ward off its
worst effects for a time; whilst the poor are at once exposed to
its pressure. This state of society exists in some sections, more
particularly in the Eastern and Middle States, and in parts of
some others, along the Atlantic sea-board; whilst all over the
west (with the exception of a few large towns), and in many other
parts of the country, an agricultural people, with habits of almost
patriarchal simplicity, prevails; and these are affected by the
fluctuations in the affairs of their artificial brethren, in proportion to the distance by which they are separated from them,
and from the influence of their more speculative habits.

If some calamity were suddenly to annihilate the commerce,
and means of existence, of some of the most populous cities in
the Eastern States, there can be no doubt that much misery
would ensue to the inhabitants of these cities, and that the effects
of the shock would be felt far and wide; but, although the
western husbandman might not be able to get so much for his
grain and cattle as he used to do, still the grain and cattle would
be produced—he would not starve.

From all this, I would infer that the agricultural emigrant,
whose destination is the Mississippi Valley, need not, from any
apparently temporal derangement of the commercial affairs of
the United States, abandon his intention of betaking himself to
that country, with the view of buying and cultivating land as a
means of subsistence.

In conclusion, I wish it to be distinctly understood that I advise no man, whatever may be his circumstances, to emigrate, either to Illinois, or to any other part of the world. I have arranged the information I possess, and have laid it before those who think of emigrating, that they may have the materials for forming a judgement for themselves. But whilst I am unwilling to advise, I may perhaps be allowed to give a caution. Let no one whose prospects are good at home rashly think of emigrating. The poor ; those who see unavoidable difficulty approaching them, and such as have families without any adequate provision for them, are the proper immigrants to a new country, where thews and sinews are convertible into wealth ; and to such many parts of the United States will afford a fitting and welcome asylum. Still it is a new country, a country of strangers, and of new habits, which form a complete and often not very pleasing contrast to those already acquired ; and *home* is the word universally used by emigrants, when speaking of their native land. Neither do I wish to recommend any particular state in the Union ; for although there are places which I prefer to others, still there are advantages and disadvantages in all. I have written chiefly about Illinois, because I happen to know more about it than the rest of the states.

THE END.